Sewing *with* Leftover Fabric

Sewing *with* Leftover Fabric

QUICK AND EASY STASHBUSTERS TO USE UP YOUR OFFCUTS AND SCRAPS

Kate Haxell

CICO BOOKS

This edition published in 2026 by CICO Books
An imprint of Ryland Peters & Small Ltd
20–21 Jockey's Fields, London WC1R 4BW
www.rylandpeters.com
Email: euregulations@rylandpeters.com

10 9 8 7 6 5 4 3 2 1

First published as *Sewing Stashbusters* in 2021. Projects in this book have previously appeared in *Sewlicious* and *Sew-licious Little Things*, both by Kate Haxell.

A CIP catalog record for this book is available from the Library of Congress and the British Library.

ISBN: 978-1-80065-664-2

Printed in China

Editor: Katie Hardwicke
Photographers: Joanna Henderson and Penny Wincer
Stylists: Sania Pell, Catherine Woram, and Luis Peral
Illustrators: Michael Hill and Carrie Hill
Technique and template illustration: Stephen Dew

Art director: Sally Powell
Head of production: Patricia Harrington
Publishing manager: Penny Craig
Publisher: Cindy Richards

The authorised representative in the EEA is
Authorised Rep Compliance Ltd.,
Ground Floor. 71 Lower Baggot Street,
Dublin, D01 P593, Ireland
www.arccompliance.com

MIX
Paper | Supporting responsible forestry
FSC www.fsc.org FSC® C106563

Contents

Introduction

If sewing is your thing, then an overflowing stash box, drawer, or closet(s) will be a familiar feature of your sewing space. You know how it happens; there's a tiny scrap left over from a toy you made last Christmas, an awkward L-shaped remnant from the last-but-three pillow you sewed, and a jar of lonely buttons collected over the years. You don't have the heart to throw them away, they're all too delicious, and you really do want to reuse and recycle where you can.

That's where this book comes to the rescue, with a collection of 25 patterns that utilize fabric oddments and scraps, perfect for using up your stash. I have included notes on fabrics I chose to use, but have given tips on easy ways to customize projects or sub out different fabrics so that you can make the most of the materials you already own. Some projects have bits you can miss out if time is tight or you want a simpler option (look out for the "miss this bit" or "excellent news" tags in the steps), and others have design-tweak ideas and fabric musings that I hope will have you pondering all sorts of possibilities while rifling through your fabric leftovers.

I've divided the book into four sections—projects for At Home, Out and About, To Wear, and For Crafters. So whether you're a newbie sewist looking for something simple and sweet (maybe try the Outdoor bunting, page 50, or Scented lavender bags, page 12), a fashionista (Pearly Peter Pan collar, page 59, or Big obi belt, page 68 should do it for you), or a master machinist (try the Washbag, page 44), there are perfectly practical projects to help use up all those beautiful fabrics you've been safely storing all this time.

Most of the projects are suitable for adventurous beginners and there are definitely some for sewing newbies, but before you begin, have a look through all the instructions for a project to make sure everything's clear. The Techniques section (pages 86–89) includes instructions for anything you are not familiar with.

Many of the projects in this book are small and simple, easy to achieve in an evening; others are equally small but will take a little more time. But either way these small things will make life good, and your sewing stash smaller. I hope you get as much pleasure from making them as I did.

Kate

CHAPTER 1

At Home

Rosy pillowcases

The matchy-matchy thing of bed linen sets doesn't appeal? It really is über-simple and seriously speedy to make your own pillowcases, and they can be as colorful and as multi-patterned as your eyes can cope with first thing in the morning. Make versions using complementary fabrics to your bedding for a bedroom that's bursting with color and pattern, but is also harmonious.

YOU'RE GOING TO NEED...

- Fabrics: see How Much Fabric?, right
- Ruler
- Rotary cutter and cutting mat, or fabric scissors
- Pins
- Iron and ironing board
- Sewing threads to match fabrics
- Sewing machine

HOW MUCH FABRIC?

Measure the width and length of a pillowcase that fits your pillow: mine is 17¾in (45cm) wide by 27¼in (69cm) long. Multiply the length by 2, so 54½in (138cm), and add 6¾in (17cm) for a flap and 3in (8cm) for a hem, so 64¼in (163cm) in total. To the width, just add 1¼in (3cm) for seam allowances, so 19in (48cm). So, 19 x 64¼in (48 x 163cm) is the size I needed to piece together.

1 Cut pieces of fabrics and sew them together, taking ⅝-in (1.5-cm) seam allowances, to make a finished piece the right size. Zigzag the seam allowances together (for durability: these pillowcases are going to get used, and so washed, a lot), and press them to one side.

2 Decide which end of the piece will be the internal flap that holds the pillow in. At that end, press under a double ⅜in (1cm) hem. At the other end, press a double 1½in (4cm) hem. Sew the hems close to the edges.

3 Some of the folding in the next couple of steps might seem counter-intuitive, but trust me… Lay the piece face down and fold back 6in (15cm) for the flap at the end with the smaller hem. Press the fold.

4 Turn the whole piece face up and open out the flap. Fold up the other end so that the hem lies against the pressed fold.

5 Fold the flap over the hem up to the pressed line: the fold will be "facing the wrong way" at this stage, but it'll be the right way on the finished pillowcase, and I always get a neater result doing it like this.

6 Pin and then sew the side seams, reversing at each end to secure the stitches. Then zigzag stitch the seam allowances. Turn the pillowcase right side out, and the flap will neatly enclose the seams. Now make your bed and lie in it!

Scented lavender bags

Lavender bags smell delicious, but often look embarrassingly twee. Why? I've no idea; there's no need for it. Make your own from scraps of your favorite fabrics, and give them little loops so you can put them on clothes hangers and make your whole closet scentilicious. The buttons help to make the lavender bag pleasingly firm, but you don't have to add them.

YOU'RE GOING TO NEED...

- Two scraps of fabric, each the size you want the lavender bag to be; mine was about 4 x 3 ¼in (10 x 8cm)
- Piece of ribbon or tape about 4in (10cm) long
- Dried lavender
- Decorative button and plain button
- Fabric scissors
- Iron and ironing board
- Pins
- Sewing threads to match fabrics
- Sewing machine
- Hand-sewing needle

1 Place the fabrics right sides together and cut out the shape you want your bag to be, remembering to cut it about ⅜in (1cm) larger all around to allow for seam allowances. If you prefer, you can make a paper template and draw around that.

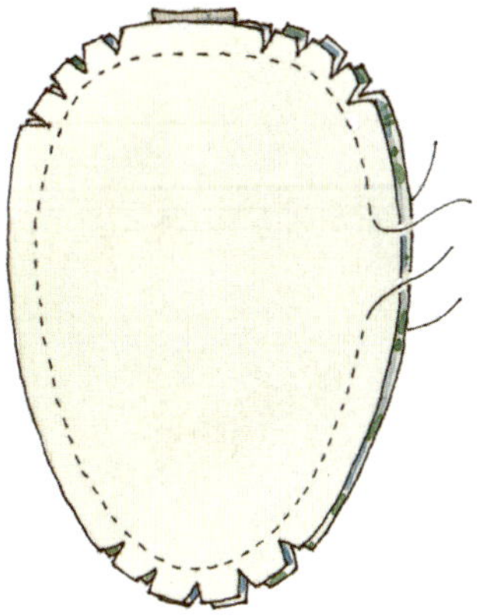

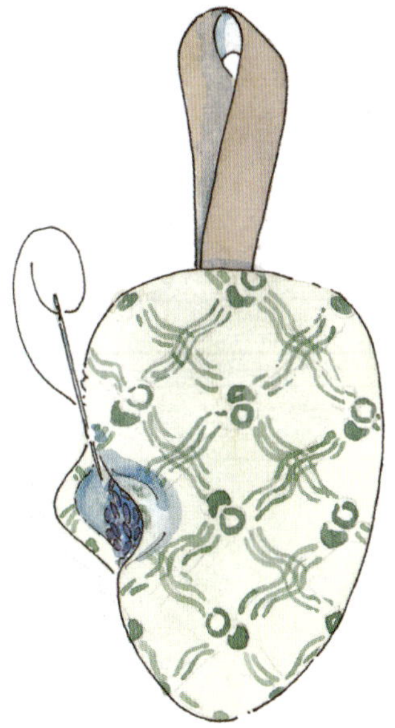

2 Fold the tape in half, overlapping the ends so that the right side of one end lies on top of the wrong side of the other end. Pin the folded tape to the right side of the front of the bag, matching the raw ends to the top edge.

3 Lay the other piece of fabric right side down on top of the first piece, with the tape in between. Taking a ⅜in (1-cm) seam allowance, sew around the edges, leaving a small gap in one side. Cut notches in the seam allowances (see page 86) around any curves.

4 Turn the bag right side out through the gap and press it flat. Fill the bag with dried lavender, then ladder stitch (see page 88) the gap closed.

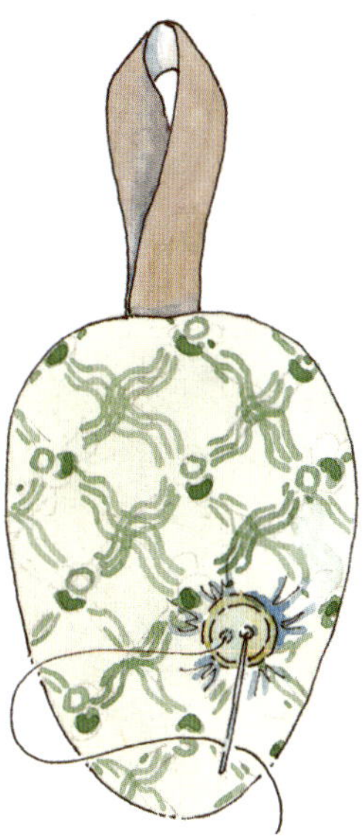

5 Thread the hand-sewing needle with a long length of thread, double it, and knot the ends. From the back, take the needle right through the bag, then thread on the decorative button. Go back down through the other hole in the button and right through to the back of the bag, then thread on the plain button. Pull the thread tight. Go back and forth through both buttons a few times, then secure the thread by looping and knotting it under the button on the back.

Hexie cushion

I've always loved the principles of hexie patchwork; the re-use of scraps of delicious fabrics, the methodical construction, the neat hand-stitching, the portability of the blocks—just the perfect craft for trains, planes, and automobiles. For this cushion I've gone for a classy two-color palette to balance out the eccentric fringing, but use a jumble of colors if that works for you. I've kept it small to make it achievable in the foreseeable future (hexie patchwork is a little slow, though for me that's one of its pleasures), but you could make a larger cushion simply by making larger hexies.

YOU'RE GOING TO NEED...

- Hexie templates (see page 92)
- Paper
- Fabric and paper scissors
- Pins
- 19 scraps of fabric measuring at least 3½in (8.5cm) square
- Basting thread: I always use ordinary sewing thread in a contrast color
- Hand-sewing needle
- Sewing threads to match fabrics
- Two pieces of medium-weight fabric at least 14in (36cm) square: I used calico
- Compasses, or a 13½-in (34-cm) diameter dinner plate to use as a template
- Sewing machine
- Iron and ironing board
- Scraps of ribbons and yarns: I used four different ribbons and three knitting yarns
- Stuffing: see Step 15

TO KNOT OR NOT TO KNOT

In a perfect world there are no knots in patchwork (apart from the basting knots). Start a seam a short way in from the corner, sew along to the corner, then sew back over these stitches and along the seam. Secure the thread by stitching back along the seam a short way. If that sounds a bit much, just start with a knot: the world isn't perfect.

Making the hexie block

1 Carefully draw around the smaller (inner) template 19 times onto paper. Cut out these hexagons VERY ACCURATELY. The success of your patchwork depends a lot on these shapes being precise. Then draw around the larger (outer) template onto the wrong side of the pieces of fabric. Cut out these fabric hexies, though you don't have to be as accurate as you were for the papers.

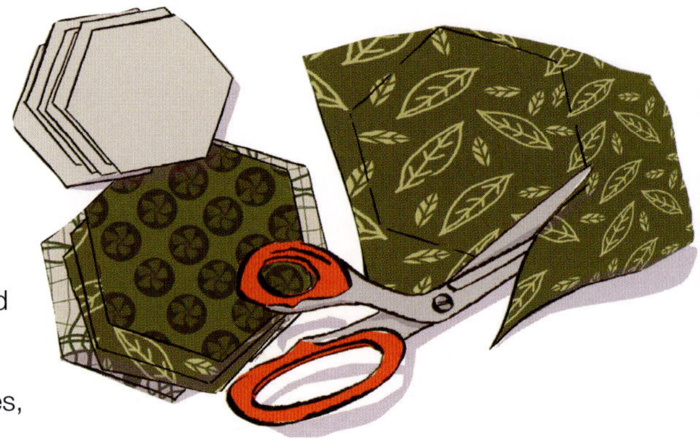

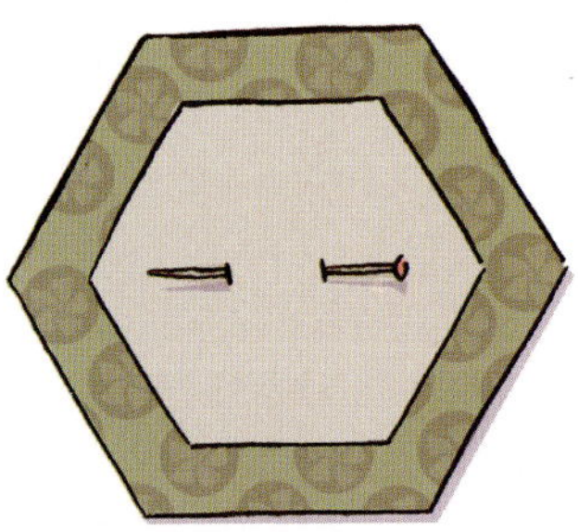

2 Thread a sewing needle—the finest you are comfortable with—and knot one end of the thread. Do this now so it's to hand when you need it. Pin a paper to the wrong side of one of the fabric pieces, centering it as accurately as you can.

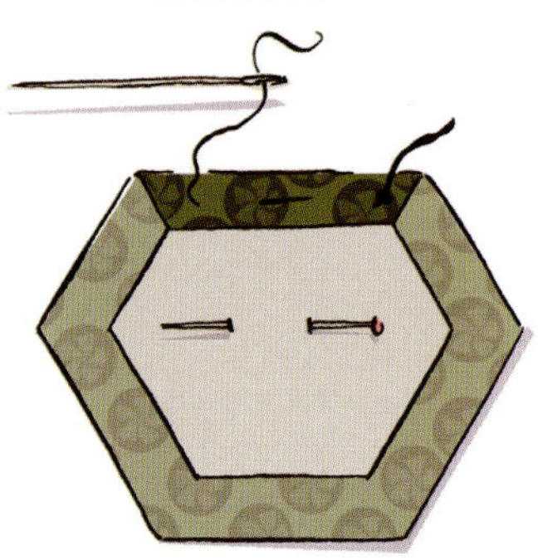

3 Fold one edge of the fabric over the paper and press it firmly with your fingers. You need to be VERY ACCURATE with all the folding and pressing so that your hexies are all the same size. From the back, baste through the fabric and paper along the folded edge, bringing the needle though to the back again a short distance before the corner.

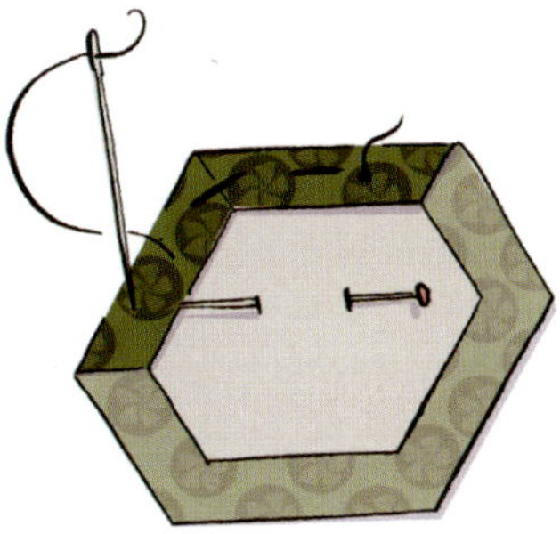

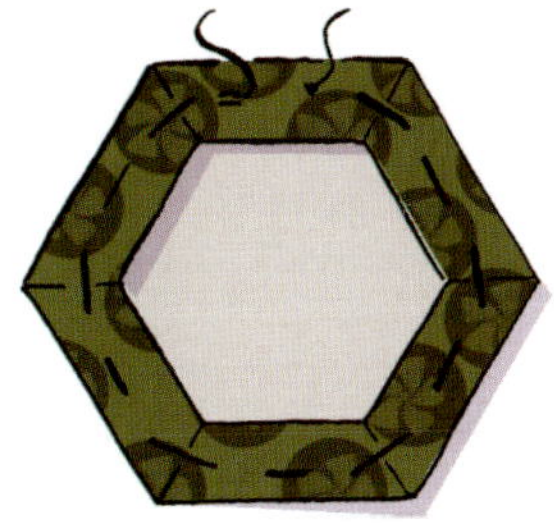

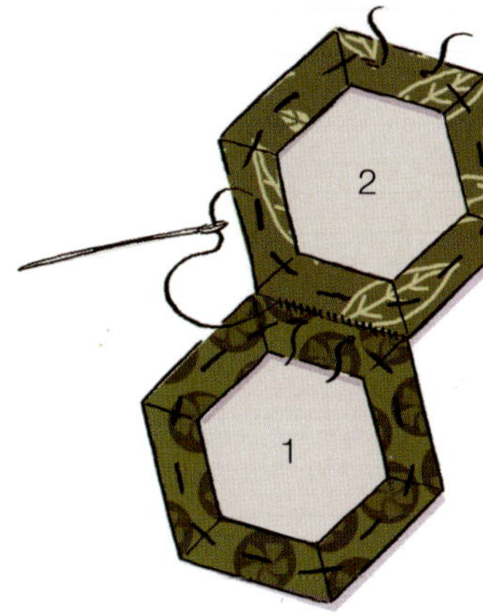

4 Fold over the adjacent edge of the fabric and finger-press it firmly, making sure that the corner is neat and sharp. Do not pull the fabric too tight or you will distort the shape of the patch. Baste along that folded edge.

5 Continue in this way right around the hexagon, folding over, pressing, and basting each edge in turn. Secure the end of the thread with a couple of backstitches through the first folded edge, stitching through the fabric only. Remove the pin. Make 18 more hexies…

6 Choose a hexie for the center and hold it right sides together with another patch, matching the edges. Using tiny whip stitches (see page 87), sew the patches together along one edge. (This illustration shows the patches flat so you can see the seam, and the patch labeled "1" is the center patch.) The stitches should go through just the very edge of the fabric, not through the paper.

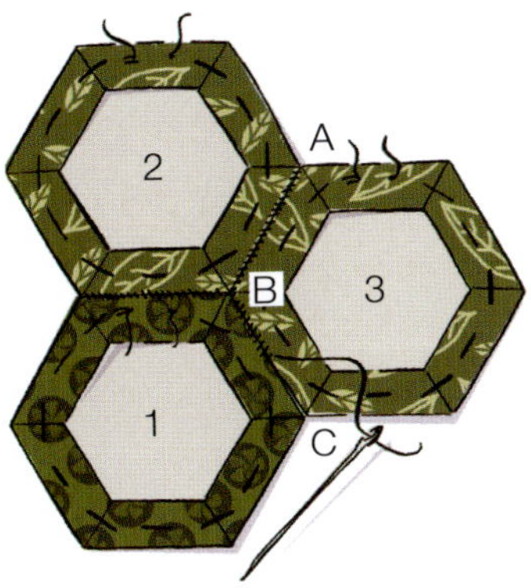

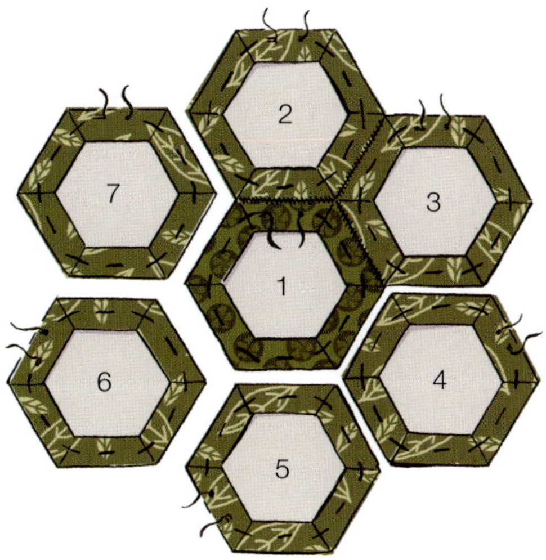

7 Hold patch 3 right sides together with patch 2 and starting at A, whip stitch them together to B, ensuring that the point at B is stitched precisely to the corner between 1 and 2. Then fold 3 so that it is right sides together with 1 (sounds tricky but it isn't, just try to crease the fabric as little as possible), and whip stitch from B to C.

8 Sew four more patches around the central patch in the same way as in Step 7, sewing each one to an edge of the previous patch and then to an edge of the central patch, and fitting them in as shown.

9 Then add another ring of 12 patches in the same way to complete the block.

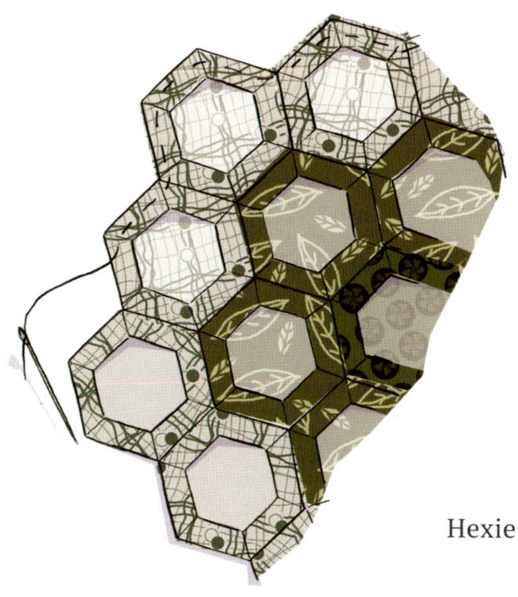

10 Press the block, then take out the basting stitches and all the papers. Do the edge patches last and do them carefully to avoid pulling on the fabric and distorting the shape, which is quite easily done (listen to the voice of bitter experience here). Baste the folded outer edges in place all round the completed patchwork.

Making the cushion

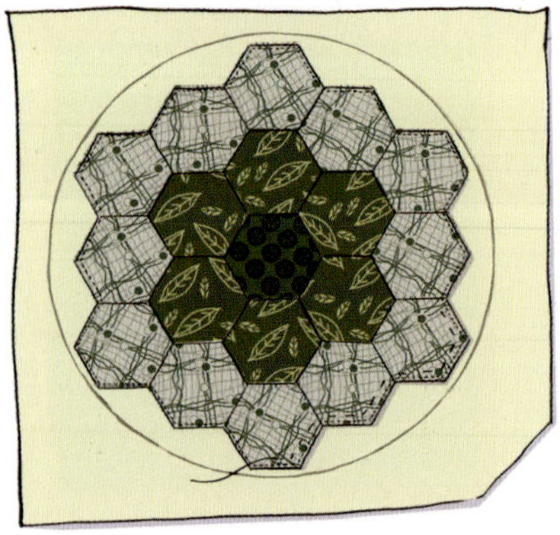

11 Draw a 13½-in (34-cm) circle on one piece of calico, but don't cut it out. Pin and then baste the hexie block centrally onto the circle, making sure it is flat and smooth. You can either hand- or machine-sew the block in place. I machine-sewed, topstitching ⅛in (3mm) in from the edge of the block and pivoting at all the corners. If you hand-sew, you can either whip stitch or blanket stitch (see page 87) around the edges. Remove the basting stitches from the outer edge of the patchwork.

12 The fringe was inspired by the idea of patchwork and is pretty much a make-it-up-as-you-go-along item. Cut lengths of ribbon about 3in (8cm) long and fold lengths of yarn into similar-sized loops. Using a straight stitch, machine-sew very slowly along the drawn line on the cushion front, feeding the loops of ribbon and yarn under the needle as you go. The loops must face inward, toward the center of the cushion, with the cut ends just protruding beyond the line. Make a few stitches to hold a loop in place, then stop with the needle down and arrange the next loop/s butted up to the previous one, and sew over those. Continue right around the cushion. If you feel the fringe is not thick enough, you can make a second row of stitching over the first one and add more loops in thin patches.

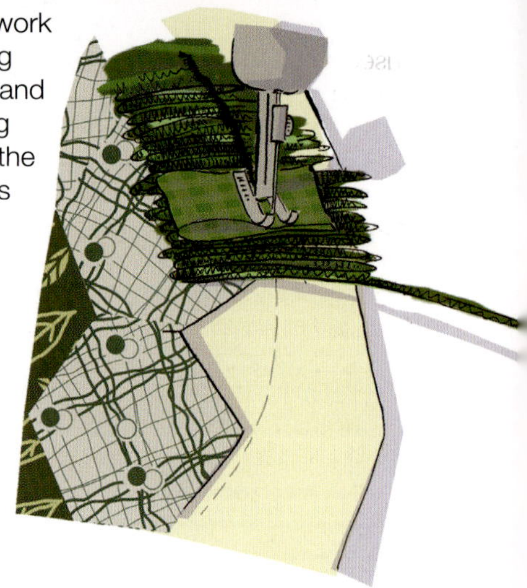

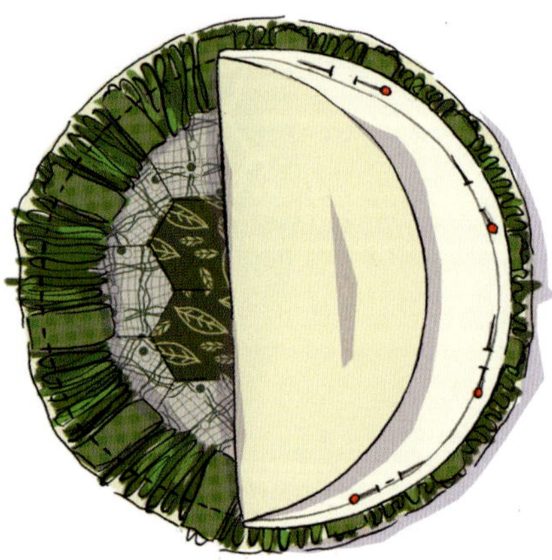

13 On the wrong side of the second piece of fabric, draw a 13½in (34cm) circle and a concentric circle ⅜in (1cm) larger. Cut out around the larger circle. Lay this right side down on top of the fringed front and pin it in place, carefully matching the drawn inner line with the line of stitching holding the fringe. Stitching just a tiny amount inside the drawn line, sew the front and back together, leaving a small gap.

14 Turn the cushion right side out through the gap and smooth out the seam with your fingers. You can snip through some of the loops of the fringe if the ribbon/yarn won't unravel.

15 Fill the cushion and ladder stitch (see page 88) the gap closed. I like feather cushions, so I raided an old square cushion for feathers to fill this one: what a nightmare! There were feathers everywhere and the only happy creatures were the cats. But once I had vacuumed me, the room, and the cushion, I liked the result, so maybe it was worth it.

Quilted bolster pillow

I like to have layers of blankets and pillows in a mix of shapes and sizes on my sofa, just because I like the way they look together. This easy-to-make bolster has trapunto "bubbles" and piping, both simple enough to do, but both optional: see the **miss this** bits in the steps (but do bear in mind that the piping helps give the gathered ends of the bolster their fab shape).

YOU'RE GOING TO NEED...

- One piece of main fabric measuring 25 x 22¾in (63 x 57cm): I used cotton
- One piece of lining fabric measuring 19½ x 22¾in (49 x 57cm): I used curtain lining
- Fabric scissors
- Iron and ironing board
- Pins
- 47in (120cm) of piping cord
- Sewing threads to match fabrics
- Sewing machine with zipper foot
- Fading fabric marker
- Topstitch or quilting sewing thread
- Hand-sewing needle
- Small, sharp embroidery scissors
- Toy stuffing
- Knitting needle or chopstick
- Bolster form (pad) measuring 17¾in (45cm) long and 21¾in (54cm) circumference
- Two 5-in (13-cm) diameter circles of felt

1 Lay the main fabric right side down. Measure down 2¾in (7cm) from each short end and press a fold right across (so the area of main fabric between the pressed folds measures 19½ x 22¾in/49 x 57cm, the same size as the lining fabric.) **Miss this** if you don't want to pipe the bolster, and cut the main fabric 1½in (4cm) shorter—so it's 23½ x 22¾in (59 x 57cm). Lay the piece of lining fabric right side down on the back of the main fabric, matching the raw edges and pressed folds of the main fabric—or centering it on the main fabric if you aren't piping.

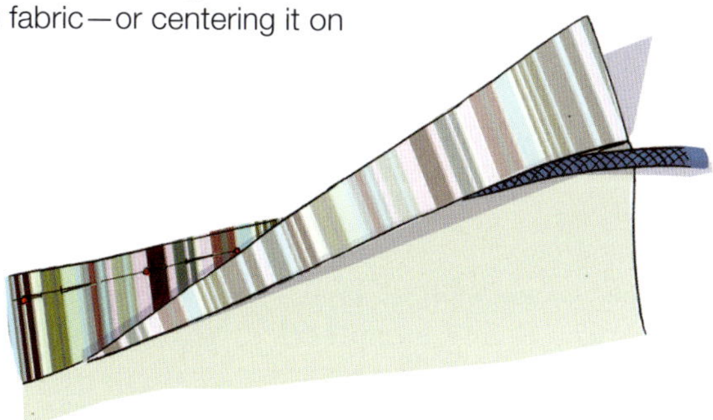

2 Cut the piping cord in half. Lay out one length of cord close to a pressed fold, approximately ⅜in (1cm) below the edge of the lining, then fold the lining and main fabric tightly over the cord and pin along the fold, as shown. You might find it easier to baste along the fold at this stage to make sure that the piping cord is tightly encased by the fabric. Obviously **miss this**, and the next step, if you aren't piping.

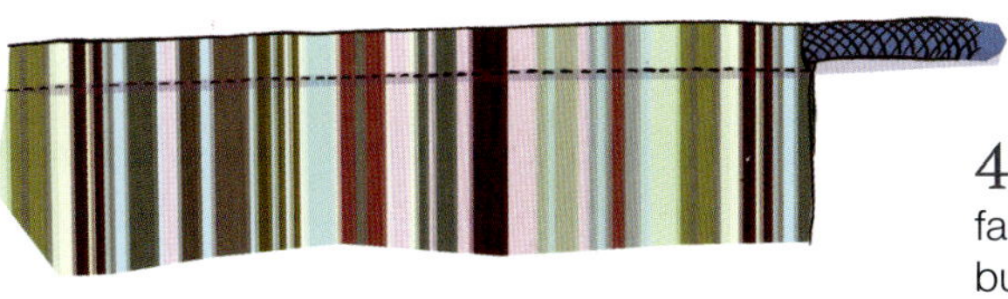

3 Fit a zipper foot to the sewing machine and sew along the pressed fold, encasing the piping. Repeat Steps 2–3 on the other pressed fold.

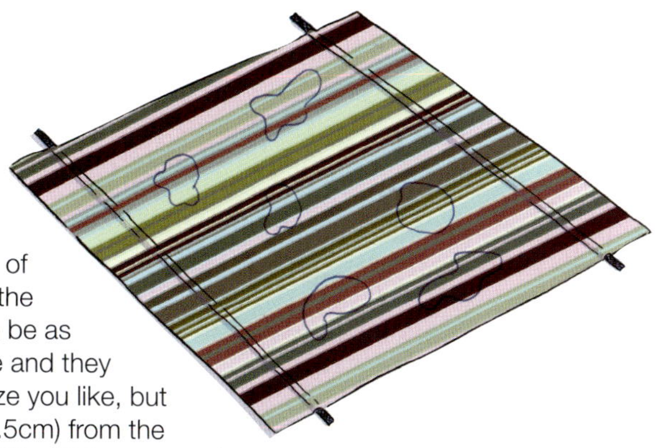

4 Using the fading fabric marker, draw bubbles on the right side of the main fabric between the lines of piping. There can be as many bubbles as you like and they can be any shape and size you like, but keep them at least 1in (2.5cm) from the raw edges of the fabric. **Miss this** step, and the next four steps, if you don't want to do the trapunto quilting.

5 Using doubled topstitch or quilting thread, work a line or tiny running stitches (see page 88) around each bubble, stitching through both layers of fabric. Start with a knot on the lining side, and finish with a few backstitches through the lining only. After this stage, make sure that the marker lines have vanished before moving on; you may find that dampening the fabric helps to remove them.

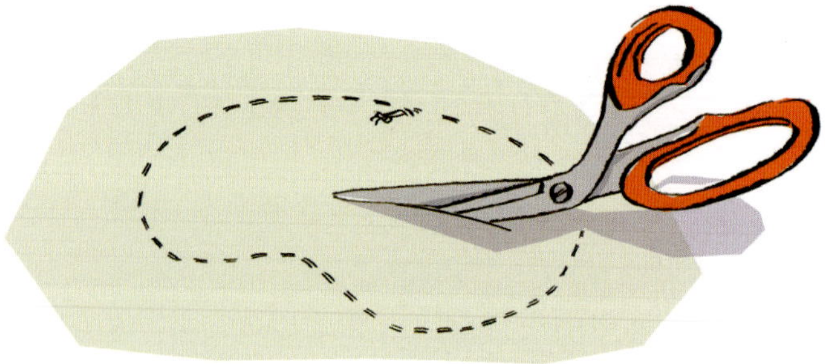

6 On the lining side, use small, sharp scissors to snip a slit in the lining fabric within each bubble outline. The cut should be at least ⅜in (1cm) in from the stitching at any point, and be very careful not to cut the main fabric.

7 Lightly stuff the bubble with toy stuffing. You can use a knitting needle or chopstick to push stuffing into the corners, but keep it soft rather than firmly packed in.

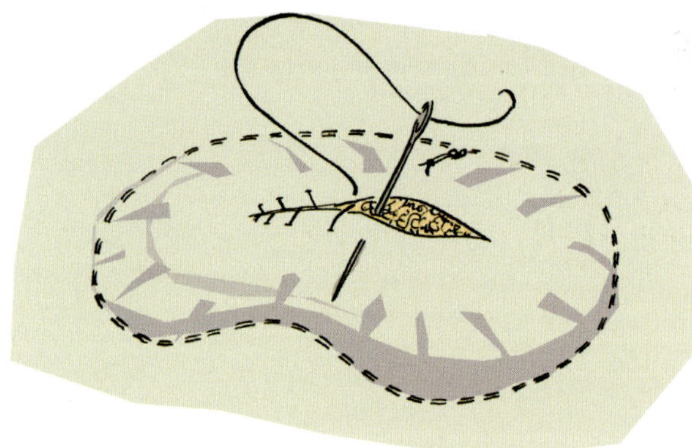

8 Sew up the slit using lacing stitch. To work this, slip the point of the needle into the slit and up through the fabric on one side, then do the same on the other side. Make stitches on alternate sides along the length of the slit, gently pulling the cut edges together as you go. Stuff and sew up every bubble.

9 Fold the fabric in half with right sides together to make a tube, matching the ends of the piping on either side. Baste the seam to make sure that the piping doesn't slip when you machine-sew. Taking a ⅝-in (1.5-cm) seam allowance, sew the seam, sewing straight over the ends of the piping at the top and bottom of the tube. Then turn under and press a ⅜-in (1-cm) hem around the raw ends.

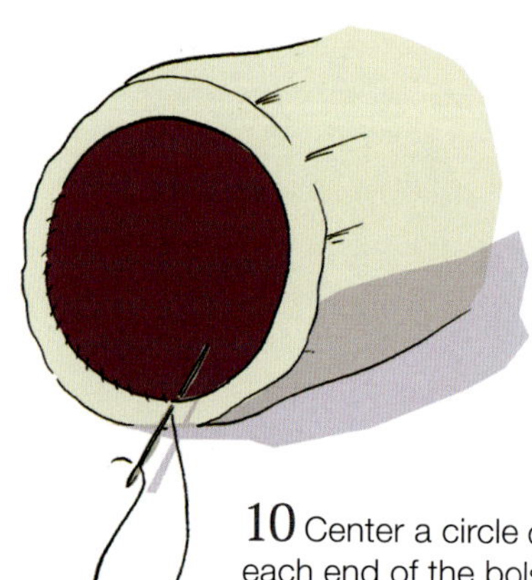

10 Center a circle of felt on each end of the bolster form (pad) and whip stitch (see page 87) it in position.

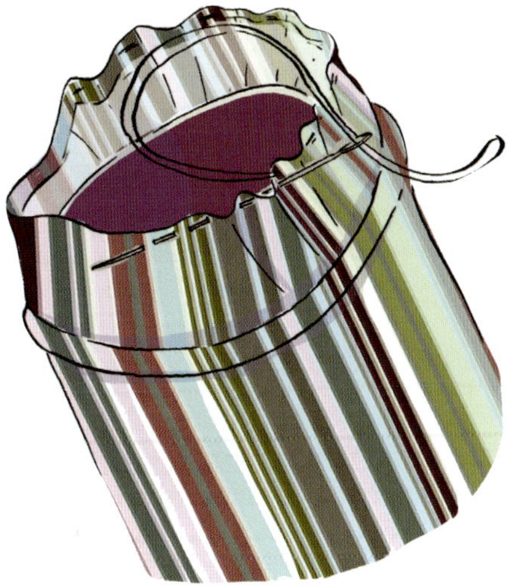

11 Turn the cover right side out and slide the bolster form (pad) into it, so that the ends of the form align with the piping. Using the strong thread, sew a line of gathering stitches around one end of the cover. Make the stitches a bit shorter on the right side than on the wrong side for the most pronounced gathers.

12 Pull on both ends of the thread to pull the gathers up as tightly as possible, then knot the threads very firmly. Thread the ends into a needle and take them down through a trough in the gathers to the back. Repeat Steps 11–12 on the other end of the cover.

Cat doorstop

A good companion for the snoozy dog (see page 23), this breed of cat might not be fat, but they are heavy and so perfectly adapted to their task of holding your door open. Made from recycled clothes and scraps of fabric, they are both thrifty and fabulous, and though their eyes might look glitteringly complicated, actually almost all of it is just stuff sewn on; there's minimal embroidery to do. And you can make your cat with different colored eyes using buttons for the centers and adding beads instead of sequins, if you prefer.

YOU'RE GOING TO NEED...

- Cat head template on page 90
- Paper for template
- Paper and fabric scissors
- Two pieces of fabric, each measuring 9in (23cm) square: I used corduroy from an old shirt
- Two pieces of felt, each measuring 3½ x 2in (9 x 5cm)
- Two gold shisha mirrors
- Tiny gold sequins
- Gold embroidery thread
- Embroidery needle
- Tiny button
- Old woolen sweater, felted (see Felting A Sweater, right)
- Pins
- Sewing threads to match fabrics
- Sewing machine
- Iron and ironing board
- Hand-sewing needle
- Basting thread: I always use ordinary sewing thread in a contrast color
- Piece of cotton fabric measuring 8 x 4in (20 x 10cm)
- Dried lentils
- Toy stuffing

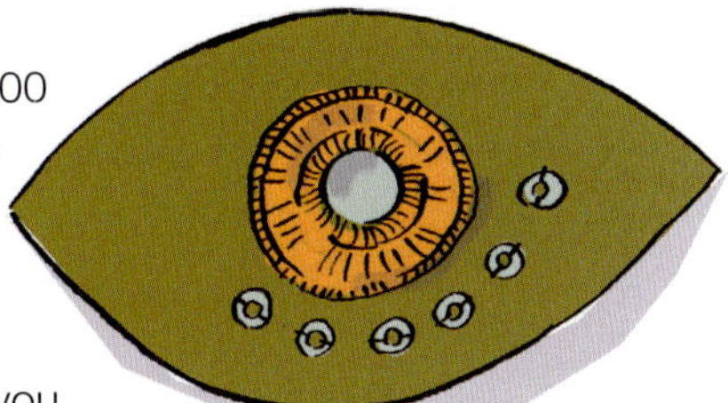

1 Enlarge the template by 200 per cent and cut out an eye. Use this eye template to cut two eyes from felt. I made slightly different designs on my cat's eyes, so he's sort of winking, but you can make your eyes identical, if you prefer. Start by sewing the mirror into the center of each eye using the gold thread. Then sew on sequins and/or embroider in chain stitch (see page 87) around the mirrors. I sewed on each sequin using two tiny straight stitches.

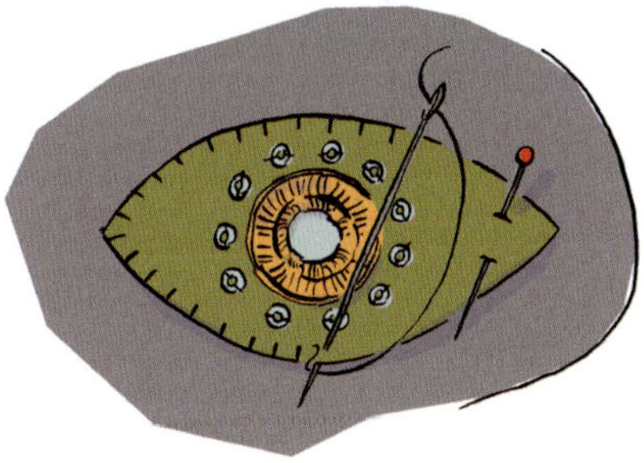

2 Using the head template, cut two heads from fabric. Position the eyes on one head on the right side of the fabric and pin them in place. Blanket stitch (see page 87) right around each eye using gold thread.

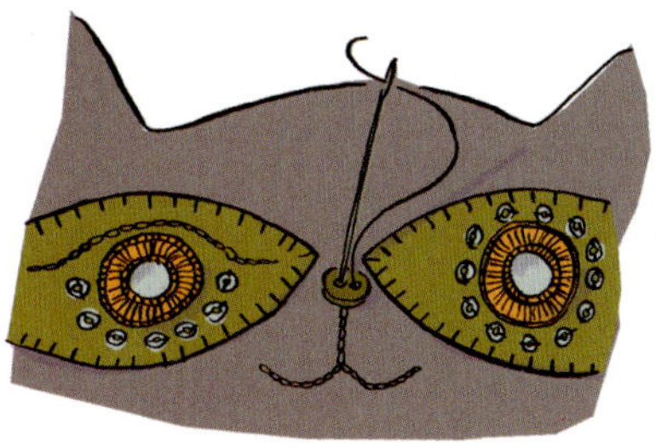

3 Following the template and using the photograph as a guide, embroider the mouth in gold chain stitch, then sew on the tiny button for the nose.

4 Pin the two head pieces right sides together. Taking a ⅜-in (1-cm) seam allowance, sew them together around the edges, leaving the bottom of the neck open. Clip the seam allowances around the curved sections (see page 86), then turn the head right side out.

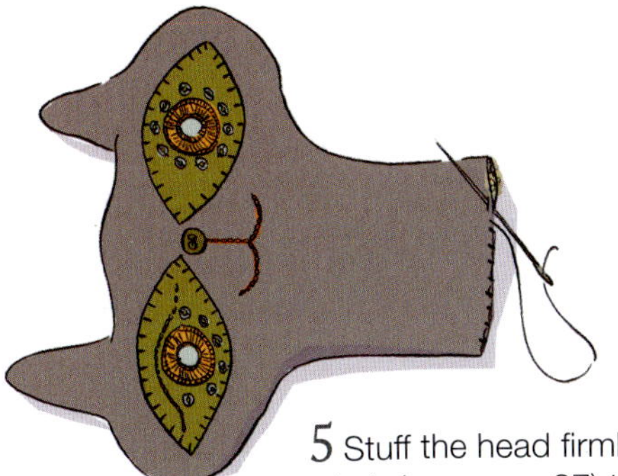

5 Stuff the head firmly and whip stitch (see page 87) the bottom of the neck closed.

6 Cut a piece of sweater, including a section of ribbed welt, measuring about 12¾ x 12in (32 x 30cm). Fold it in half right sides together and pin, placing a pin halfway down the welt and 4in (10cm) from the fold. Set the sewing machine to a tight zigzag stitch and sew a gently curving line from the outside edge of the bottom up to the pin, as shown.

FELTING A SWEATER

If you have a beautiful sweater—or cardigan, or tank—that you have inadvertently ruined by hot-washing it, then this is the perfect way to give it a new lease of life. If you're more careful with your laundry than that (I am, nowadays...), then you'll need to hunt for a sweater to ruin. The sweater needs to be 100 percent wool that hasn't been treated to make it machine washable: check the label and if it says "wash by hand," or "cool temperature wash," then you're good to go. And it's even better if it has a deep, ribbed welt.

You can felt in the washing machine, but I prefer to do it by hand as I get more control over the result: an overly-felted sweater can be too thick and stiff to make a nice cat from. You're going to need a sink, hot water, cold water, rubber gloves, laundry detergent, and about 45 minutes. Firstly, fill the sink with the hottest running water available. Put on the gloves (to avoid scalding your hands), and mix into the hot water as much detergent as you'd use for a washer-load of laundry. Plunge the sweater into the water and start rubbing it between your hands. Rub one section, then move on to the next to felt it as evenly as possible all over. After about 30 minutes it should have thickened and the stitches blurred as the wool has felted. Drain the sink and fill it with cold water, then rinse the sweater thoroughly. If it isn't felted to your liking, then repeat the process.

If all that sounds like too much hard work (though it's very good for toning the upper arms), put the sweater in an old pillowcase (to avoid fibers clogging your washing machine), throw it in a hot wash, and cross your fingers.

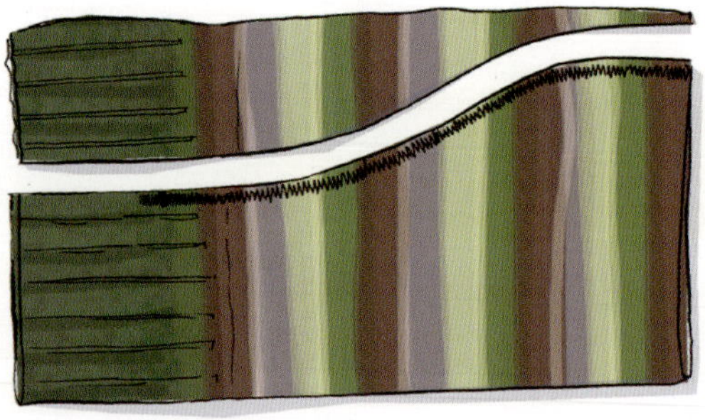

7 Cut off the excess fabric, cutting straight up from the top of the line of stitching to the top of the welt.

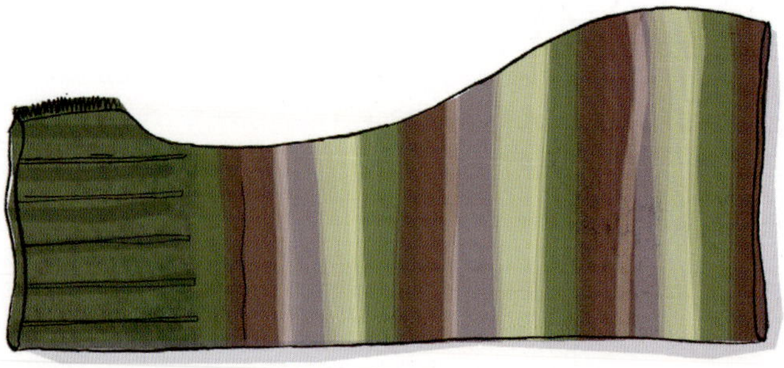

8 Turn the sweater right side out, then sew up the open part of the welt using a tight zigzag stitch as before. Test that the cat sweater welt fits snugly around the cat's neck, and take it in a bit more if need be.

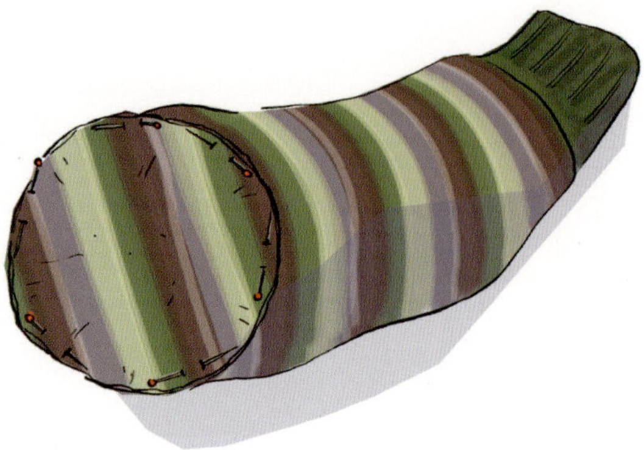

9 Cut a circle of felted sweater measuring 4in (10cm) in diameter. Turn the tube of cat sweater wrong side out again, and pin the circle into the base. Ease the two pieces to fit; you may find it easiest to quickly baste the circle in place, rather than trying to sew with all the sticking-out pins. Using the tight zigzag stitch as before, sew the base in place. Turn the cat sweater right side out.

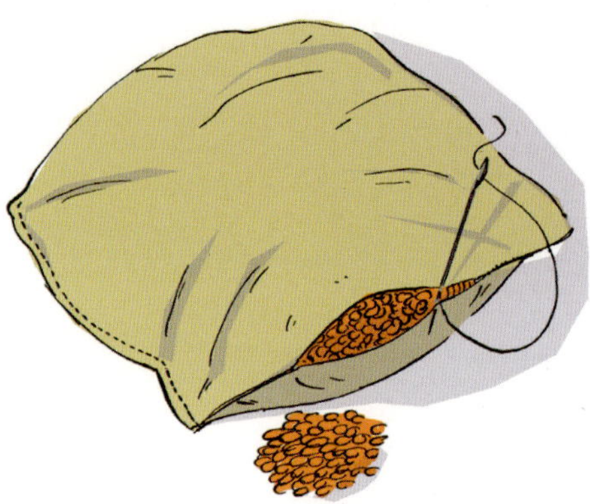

10 Fold the piece of cotton fabric in half and machine-sew the sides to make a small bag, leaving part of one side open. Fill the bag with dried lentils, packing in as many as you can, then hand-sew the gap closed.

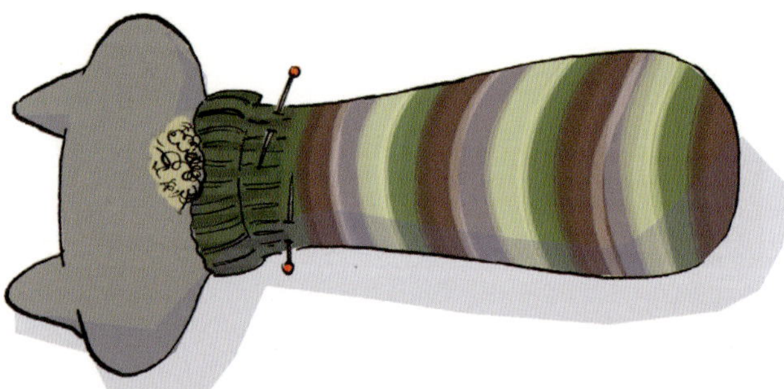

11 Push the bag of lentils into the bottom of the cat sweater and pack in stuffing around it so that it's held firmly in place. Try to keep the base of the cat sweater as flat as possible. Stuff the sweater firmly up to the welt. Fold the welt over in half, then fold the top layer back up on itself. Push the cat's neck into the sweater and pin it in place through the single underlayer of the welt into the neck. If need be, add more stuffing to keep the cat's head from drooping.

12 Thread a needle with sewing thread, double it, and knot the ends. Sewing about halfway up the underlayer of the welt, backstitch (see page 87) the welt to the neck all around. Make the stitches go deeply into the neck so that the head is very firmly attached to the sweater (these cats tend to get picked up by their pointy ears, and you don't want the head coming off in your hand…). Fold the top layer of the welt down to cover the stitching.

Sausage dog draft excluder

If you live in an efficiently insulated house, just pretend it's drafty then you have an excuse for a fabulously retro doggie to snooze in front of your door or along your windowsill. Vincent (so called because he's orange) is completely adjustable in length to fit any door or window. And he does make an excellent child's toy (not for babies due to the buttons and pom-pom) if you really can't justify him as a draft excluder.

YOU'RE GOING TO NEED...

- Head, tail, ear, and leg templates on page 93
- Paper for templates
- Ruler and pencil
- Sticky tape
- Paper and fabric scissors
- Two pieces of fabric measuring 10in (25cm) by the length of your door/window plus ¾in (2cm) for the body, two pieces measuring 16 x 4in (40 x 10cm) for the ears (use a contrast fabric for the inner ear), and eight pieces measuring 6¾ x 4in (17 x 10cm) for the legs: I used needlecord for the body, outer ears, and legs, and quilting cotton for the inner ears
- Two large and two small buttons for eyes, and four large buttons to hold legs on
- Scraps of felt
- Fabric marker pen
- Pins
- Hand-sewing needle
- Sewing threads to match fabrics
- Sewing machine
- Iron and ironing board
- Small pom-pom: I cut one from a piece of furnishing trim
- Toy stuffing
- Very long sewing needle, such as a doll needle
- Strong sewing thread, such as buttonhole thread

1 Enlarge all the templates by 200 percent. Decide on the length you want your finished dog to be and cut a strip of paper measuring that length by 4¾in (12cm). Tape the dog head and tail to the strip to make a complete template the right length. Cut out two bodies, four front legs, and four back legs (remembering to fold the fabric or flip the templates to get right-hand and left-hand pieces for each). Fold the ear fabrics in half and pin the straight edge of the template to the fold, then cut out a folded ear from each piece.

2 Make eyelids for your dog by laying the large eye buttons on the felt and drawing around part of them to make a semicircle, then cutting out the shapes, adding a small border to the circumference. I've made quite large eyelids, as Vincent is definitely a snoozy dog.

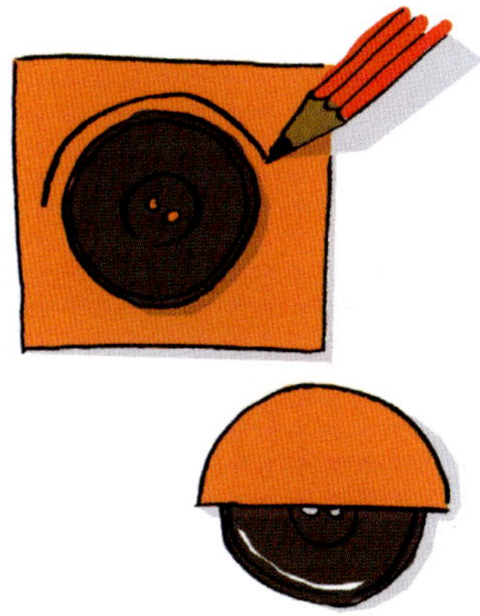

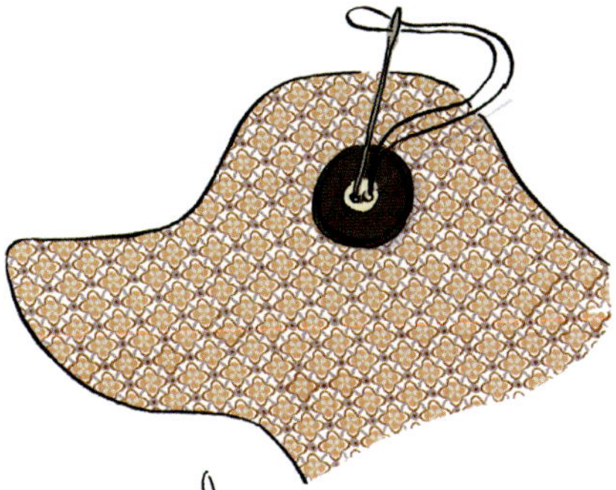

3 Sew the button eyes to the middle of the rounded part of the dog's head. Sew on a larger button topped by a smaller button: I've used a brown button topped by a pearl one for rather sleepy eyes, but you could use a colored button topped by a black one for bright eyes.

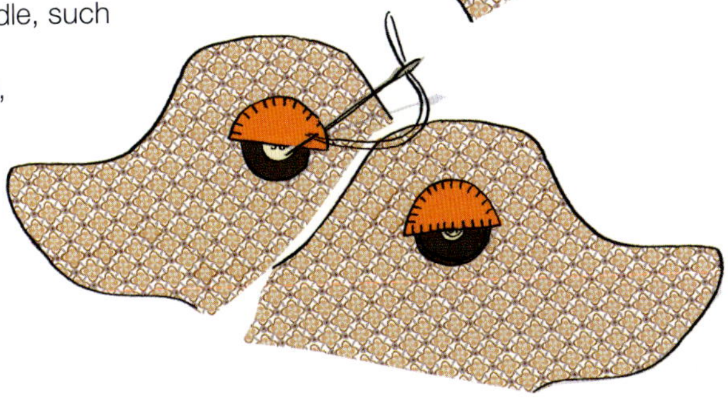

4 Pin an eyelid in position over each eye. Using doubled sewing thread to match the felt and starting at one end of the curve, blanket stitch (see page 87) the curve of the eyelid to the head. Then carry the stitching on across the straight edge of the eyelid and secure the thread on the back of the head.

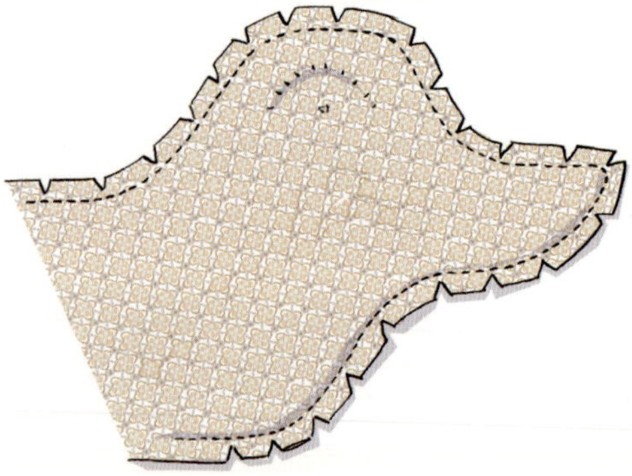

5 Pin the two body pieces right sides together. Taking a ⅜-in(1-cm) seam allowance, machine-sew all around, leaving a small gap in the tummy for turning through. Clip notches into the seam allowances around all curved sections (see page 86), then turn the dog right side out and press the seam open.

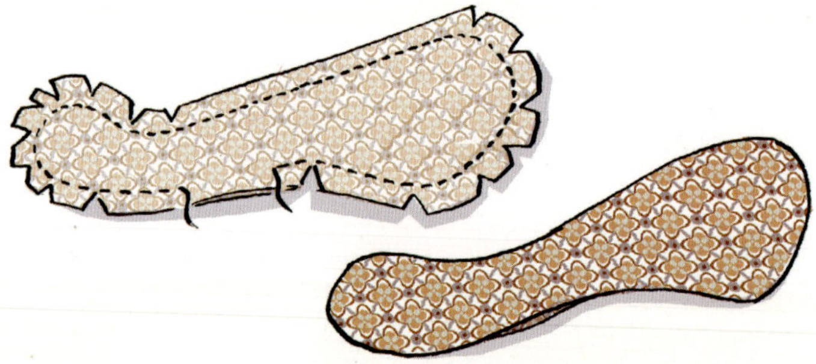

6 Pair up the leg pieces, right sides together, to make two front and two back legs. Sew seams, leaving a small gap in one edge, and clip seam allowances as for the body (see Step 5), then turn right side out and press.

7 Open the inner and outer ear pieces out flat (they should each look like an elongated figure 8), and, right sides together, sew seams and clip seam allowances as for the body (see Step 5), leaving a gap near the middle. Turn right side out and press the ears flat, then ladder stitch (see page 88) the gap closed.

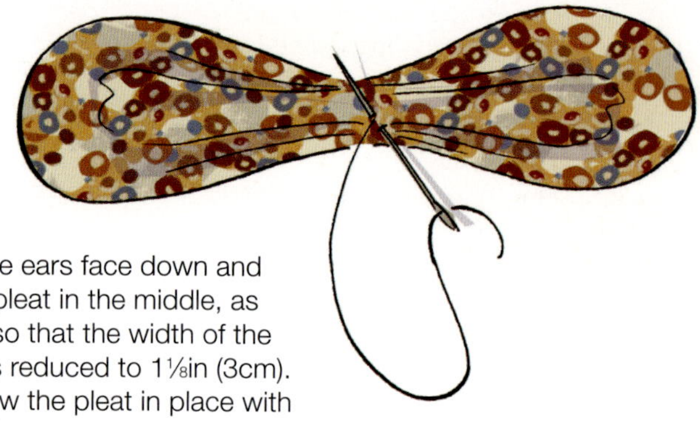

8 Lay the ears face down and make a pleat in the middle, as shown, so that the width of the middle is reduced to 1⅛in (3cm). Hand-sew the pleat in place with tiny stitches that aren't visible on the other side.

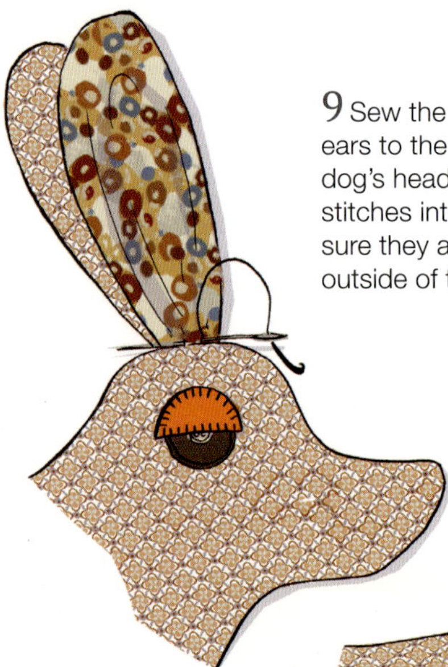

9 Sew the pleated middle of the ears to the seam on the top of the dog's head, again using small stitches into the pleat, but making sure they aren't visible on the outside of the ears.

10 Sew a small pom-pom to the tip of the snout to make a cute nose.

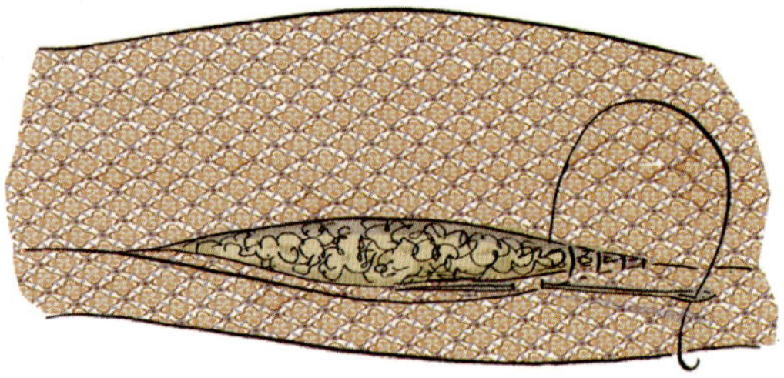

11 Stuff the body and legs with toy stuffing: stuff the head, neck, and tail very firmly, but fill the body of the dog more lightly. Stuff all the legs firmly. Ladder stitch all the gaps closed.

12 Thread the long needle with a long length of strong thread, double it, and knot the ends. To sew on the front legs, first make an anchoring stitch in one side of the chest at the spot marked by a star on the template. Then push the needle straight through the body so that it emerges on the other side in exactly the same spot (or close to it; your dog won't stand up so it doesn't matter if he's a bit wonky legwise).

13 Thread on a front leg, taking the needle through the leg at the starred spot on the template, then go through one hole in a button, back down through the other hole, then take the needle back through the body where it came through the first time. Thread on the other leg then a button, then take the needle through all the elements (button, leg, body, leg, button) several times. Finish and secure the thread on the opposite side of the body to the starting knot. Repeat the process to attach the back legs.

Patchwork tea cozy

You can't beat the all-time classic cozy; the tea cozy. But you can have some fun with it. This version is made from simple-to-sew wonky strippy patchwork, topped with perky pom-poms. It's an ideal project for using up scraps of lovely leftover fabrics.

YOU'RE GOING TO NEED...

- Fabric and batting (wadding): see How Much Fabric?, below
- Pom-pom trimming
- Paper for template
- Paper scissors and fabric scissors
- Tape measure
- Iron and ironing board
- Pins
- Sewing threads to match fabrics
- Sewing machine with zipper foot
- Hand-sewing needle

HOW MUCH FABRIC?

- You need to start by making a paper pattern for your tea cozy. Measure right around your teapot, including the spout and handle, and divide that measurement in half. Measure from the top of the lid to the base. Add 1½in (4cm) ease and seam allowances to each measurement. Using these final measurements, draw a dome shape on paper. Cut it out, trace around it to draw another the same, then tape them together to make a muslin to try on your teapot. Adjust the fit if necessary.
- You'll need two pieces of lining fabric and two pieces of batting (wadding) large enough for your paper pattern, a selection of fabric pieces as wide or as tall as the pattern, and enough pom-pom trim to go around the top edge of the dome.

1 Make a paper pattern as explained in How Much Fabric?, below left. Cut two lining pieces and two batting (wadding) pieces using your paper pattern. I then used a lining piece as a template for the patchwork outer cozy, because I found it easier to pin in place, but you can use the paper pattern if you prefer.

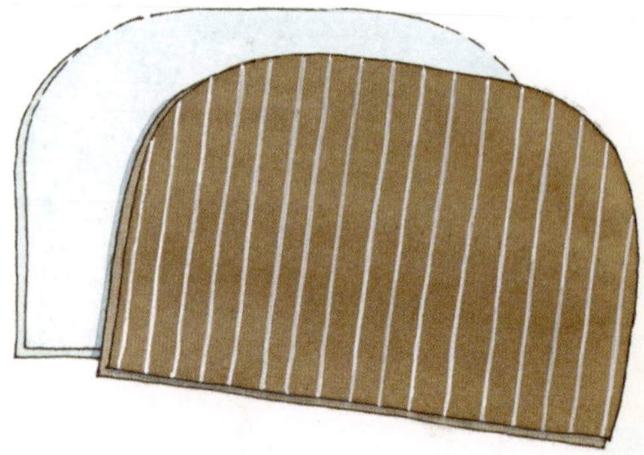

2 Taking ⅜-in (1-cm) seam allowances, sew wonky strips together to make a rough rectangle that's a little larger all around than a lining piece. Cut the first strip, sew it right sides together to one edge of a larger piece of fabric, press the seam allowances open, and then cut the larger piece down to make a wonky strip the size you want. Continue in this way until the patchwork is the size you need. Make a second patchwork the same way: I made one with vertical strips and one with horizontal strips.

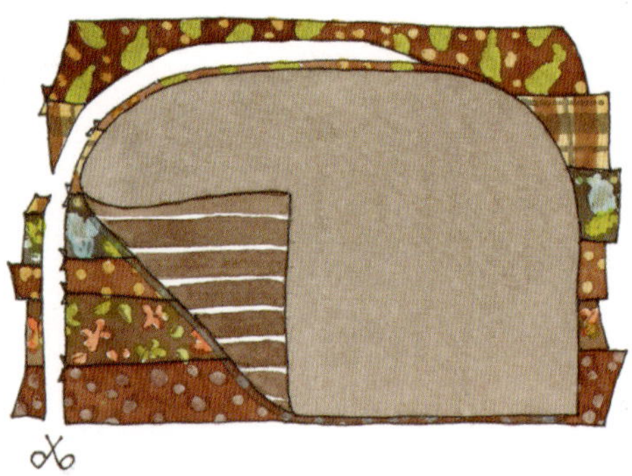

3 Pin the lining or paper pattern to the patchworks and use it as a template to cut out two outer tea cozies.

4 Lay one outer piece right side up. Starting on one side of the dome, ¾in (2cm) up from the straight bottom edge, baste (tack) the pom-pom trim to the patchwork, positioning the edge of the flat braid so that it is within the ⅜in (1cm) seam allowance. Stop ¾in (2cm) before the straight edge on the other side of the dome.

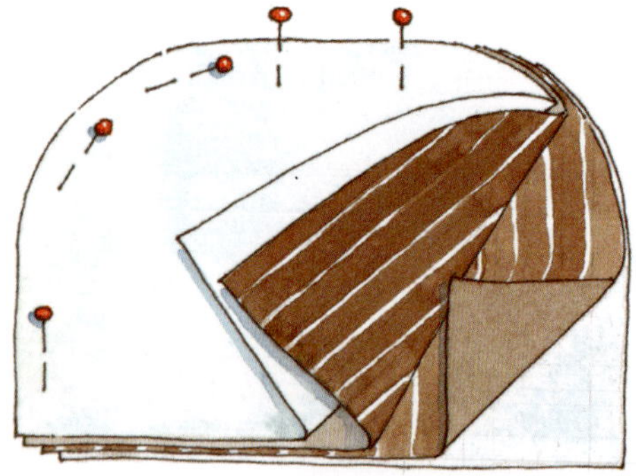

5 Lay the second patchwork piece right side down over the first, matching all raw edges. Pin the layers together. Sew the dome seam, taking a ⅜-in (1-cm) seam allowance and using a zipper foot so that the foot doesn't catch on the bobbles. Turn the outer cozy right side out and check that the bobbles look good. If anything needs fixing, do it now, unpicking and re-sewing parts of the seam if need be.

6 Pair up the lining pieces with the batting pieces, placing the batting on the wrong side of the lining. Treat these pieces as a single layer from now on. Pin the lining pieces right sides together and sew the dome seam, taking a ½-in (1.2-cm) seam allowance and leaving a 2-in (5-cm) gap at the center top: you can mark the position of this with pins before you sew. Trim the seam allowances down to ¼in (5mm), except across the gap.

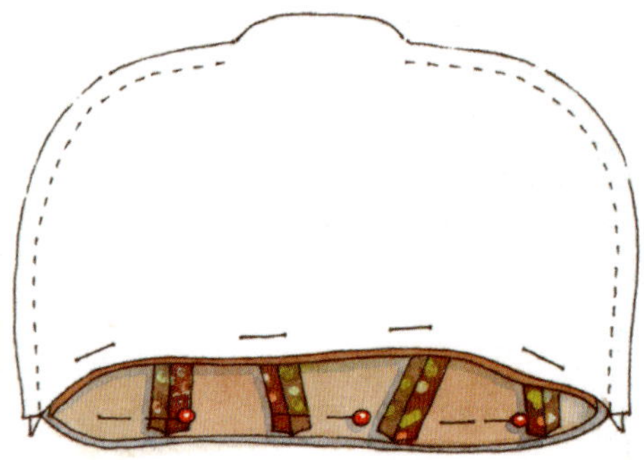

7 Slip the right-side out outer cozy into the inside-out lining, matching the bottom raw edges. Pin and then sew right around the bottom edge, taking a ⅜-in (1-cm) seam allowance.

8 Turn the cozy right side out through the gap in the lining, pulling the outer cozy through, then continuing to pull until the whole thing is right side out. Press the seams flat, pressing under the seam allowances across the gap. Ladder stitch (see page 88) the gap closed.

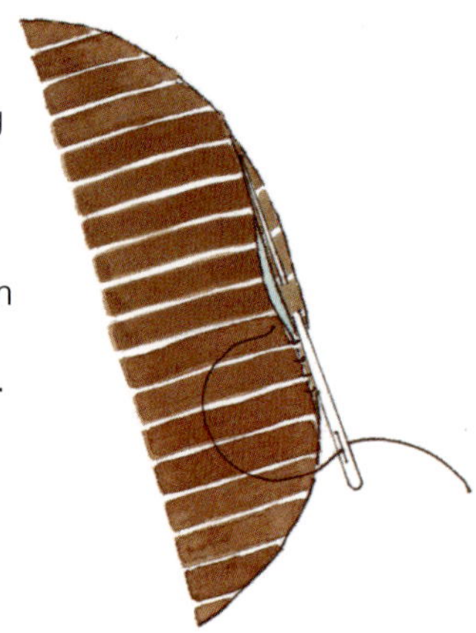

9 Tuck the lining inside the outer cozy and press the bottom edge. Topstitch around it, sewing ⅛in (2–3mm) in from the edge.

Double-sided oven glove

This is my preferred style of oven glove: I don't like two separate mittens as I always manage to drop one just after I've opened the oven door. You can buy special heat-resistant batting (wadding), and choosing washable fabrics will make your gloves practical as well as lovely to look at.

YOU'RE GOING TO NEED...

- Two pieces of sturdy fabric and one piece of heat-resistant batting (wadding) measuring 8 x 33½in (20 x 85cm) and two pieces of sturdy fabric and of heat-resistant batting Measuring 8in (20cm) square: I used ticking for the fabric
- Two pieces of decorative fabric measuring 8in (20cm) square for the front of the mitts, and one piece measuring 5 x 7in (5 x 18cm) for the loop: I used quilting cotton
- Tape measure
- Fading fabric marker
- 8-in (20-cm) diameter plate, or compasses
- Fabric scissors
- Iron and ironing board
- Pins
- Sewing threads to match fabrics
- Sewing machine

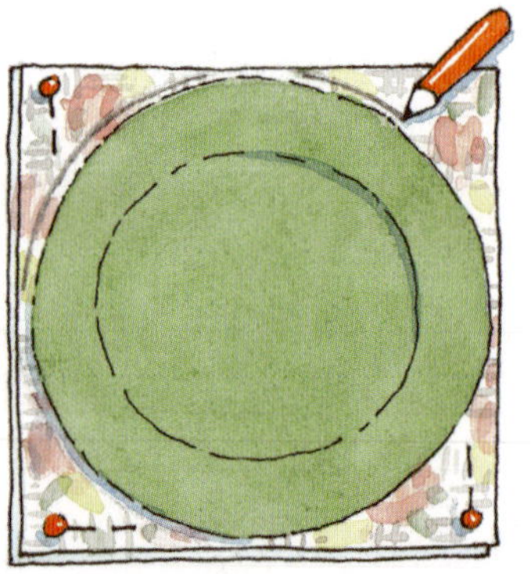

1 Pin the 8in (20cm) squares of fabric and batting (wadding) together in pairs. Draw around the plate, or use compasses, to round off two adjacent corners of each square. Also round off the corners at both ends of the long pieces of fabric and batting. Trim off the corners following the curved line.

2 Lay a rounded square of sturdy fabric right side up on a rounded square of batting and then lay a rounded square of decorative fabric right side down on top of the sturdy fabric. Pin the layers together and, taking a ⅜-in (1-cm) seam allowance, sew across the top straight edge.

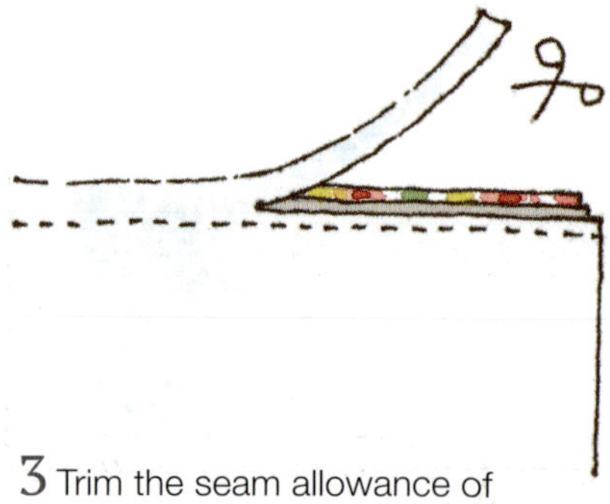

3 Trim the seam allowance of the batting down to just ⅛in (2–3mm) from the stitching.

4 Fold the decorative fabric over to lie right side up on the batting, rolling the top edge to the back by a tiny amount so that none of the sturdy fabric shows on the right side. Press the seam flat. Trim off any excess batting and sturdy fabric around the bottom edge. Repeat steps 2 and 3 with the remaining rounded squares.

5 Right side in, fold the loop strip in half lengthwise. Taking a ⅜-in (1-cm) seam allowance, sew the long edge. Turn the tube right side out (see page 86). With the seam along one edge, press the tube flat.

6 Fold the loop strip in half and baste (tack) it to one of the long pieces, in the middle of one straight edge. Make sure that the loop is square to the edge, and match the ends of the loop to the raw edge of the long piece.

7 Lay the long piece of batting flat. Lay one of the long pieces of sturdy fabric right side up on top of the batting. Then position one mitt section, decorative fabric right side up, at each end of the long piece of fabric. Finally, lay the other long piece of fabric right side down on top of the whole lot. Pin all the layers together.

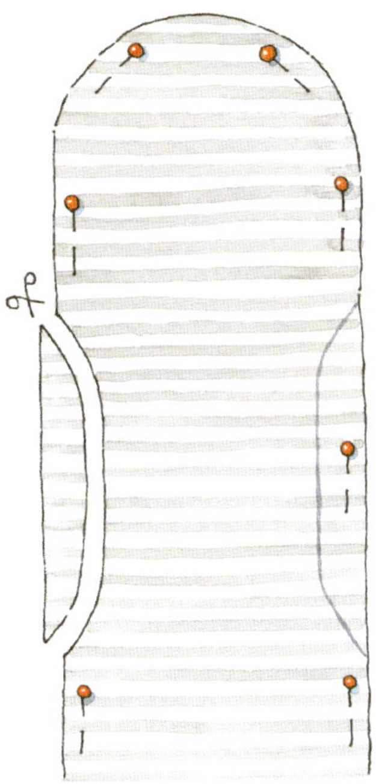

8 At this stage, you can if you want (and I did) shape the strap of the oven glove between the two mitts. I made mine thinner in the middle, just so that it was a little more elegant. Draw shaping onto the fabric using a fabric marker, remembering to include a ⅜-in (1-cm) seam allowance, then cut it out. If you do this, remember to reposition the loop before cutting out the shaping.

9 Sew right around the oven glove, leaving a 4½-in (12-cm) gap in one long edge. Trim the batting back as in Step 3. Turn the glove right side out through the gap and then ladder stitch the gap closed (see page 88). Press the glove flat.

CHAPTER 2

Out and About

Yo-yo storage pouch

Both a stash buster and a stash holder: how good can a simple bag get? One thing that all campers need is storage to stash their stuff in and keep a tiny tent tidy, so make as many bags as you need to organize your unmentionables, wash kit, pjs, wooly hat and scarf (just in case)... This is a big bag, but you can make yours any size you like. The yo-yos are optional—without them you can whiz up a bag in under half-an-hour—but they are rather lovely, and really much easier to make than they might look (check out the **Excellent News** bits in the steps).

YO-YO SIZES

Remember that a yo-yo will be the size of the smaller, inner circle; it's easiest to work out the sizes and positions you want for the yo-yos by placing just the smaller circles on the bag piece and taking a photo, before ironing the circles onto the larger ones.

YOU'RE GOING TO NEED...

- Template on page 94
- Paper for templates
- Paper scissors and fabric scissors
- Two pieces of main fabric and two pieces of lining fabric, each measuring 20 x 14in (50 x 35cm): I used medium-weight cotton, but you can use anything reasonably sturdy
- Fabrics for yo-yos: I used 6in (15cm), 8in (20cm), and 9½in (24cm) circles for the gathered parts and 3¾in (9cm), 5in (13cm), and 6in (15cm) circles for the contrast inners: I used lightweight cotton, you don't want anything thick or the yo-yos won't gather nicely
- Fusible webbing the size of the contrast inner circles
- Iron and ironing board
- Sewing threads to match fabrics
- Hand-sewing needle
- Sewing machine with free-motion embroidery function (if you want to do the embroidery...)
- Variegated machine embroidery thread (see above...)
- Pins
- Decorative buttons (if you want them...)
- 8in (20cm) zipper: I used a chunky vintage one with a big metal ring that I can hang up my bag from

1 Enlarge the template by 200 percent (you'll have to do this on several sheets of paper and tape them together to make a big bag), or draw your own template: the top straight edge needs to be the length of your zipper tape. Cut out two main pieces and two linings: remember that you need mirror image pieces, so either fold the fabric and cut through two layers, or flip the template before cutting the second piece.

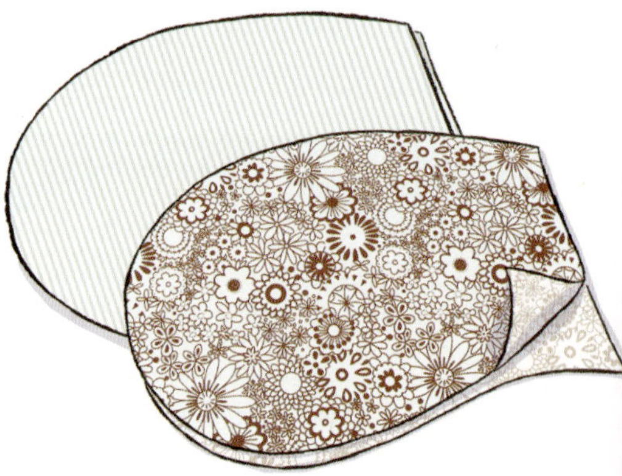

To make the yo-yos

2 Cut circles of fusible webbing the size you want the finished yo-yos to be and iron them on to the back of the pieces of contrast inner fabric. Cut out all the circles you'll need.

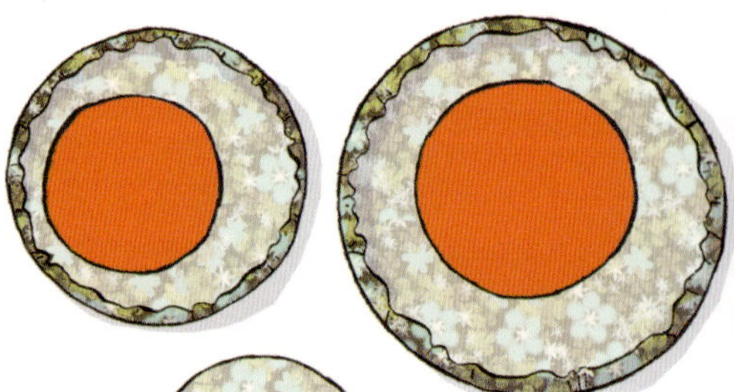

3 Peel the paper backing off the webbing and iron a small circle onto the wrong side of each larger circle. You can position the small circles off-center, as here, but make sure that they are at least 1in (2.5cm) from the edge of their big circle. Press under a very narrow hem all around the edge of each large circle. **Excellent News:** these hems don't have to be even as it doesn't matter if your circle is less than perfectly circular.

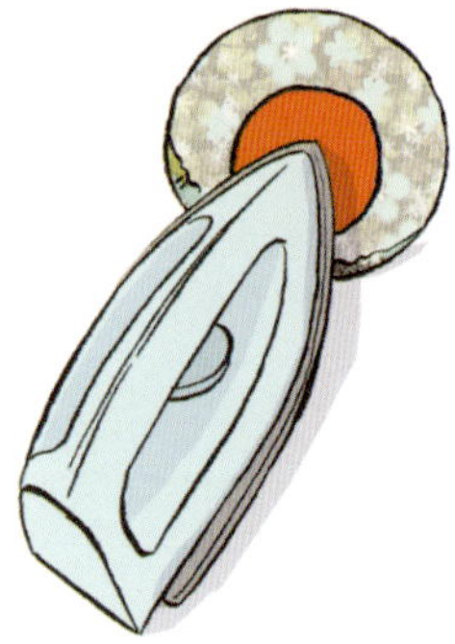

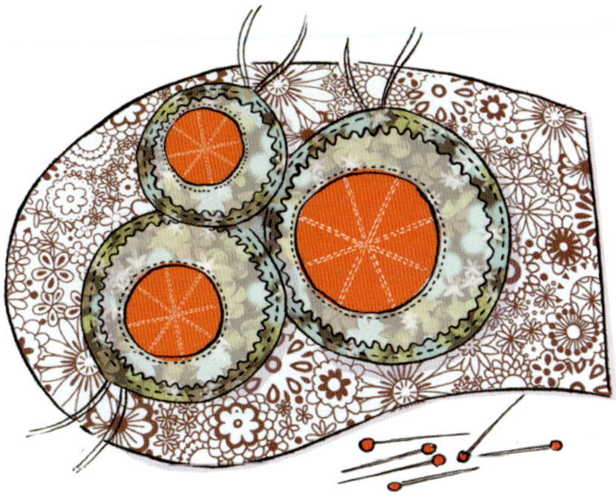

4 I embellished the middle of my yo-yos by scribbling on them with free-motion embroidery and variegated thread. You could leave yours plain, use a print fabric, use hand-embroidery stitches (see pages 87–89), sew on buttons or patches; whatever you want really.

5 Using a long length of doubled sewing thread, work a row of running stitches around the hem of each circle, starting and ending on the right side. **More Excellent News:** the stitches don't need to be even or neat, though they shouldn't be too long—about ¼in (6mm) is good. Leave a long tail of thread hanging free at the end of the stitches.

6 Pin the yo-yos onto the bag front piece: it doesn't matter if the larger circles overlap. Set the sewing machine to a small straight stitch (if you did machine embroidery in Step 4, remember to raise the feed dogs), and sew around the edge of each smaller circle. **Yet More Excellent News:** the stitched circles don't have to sit smoothly against the fabric circles, or be perfectly round.

7 One yo-yo at a time, pull on the tail of the gathering thread (the one you left hanging free in Step 5) and the starting knot end to gather up the edge of the yo-yo. Even out the gathers a bit (**Another Piece Of Excellent News:** it doesn't matter if the gathers aren't THAT even), and make sure that the inner circle is lying flat. (If you pull up the gathers too tight, the inner circle will bunch up and the bag piece won't lie flat.) Tie the tail and knot end together in a firm double knot.

8 Thread the ends of the gathering threads into a needle and take them down through a trough in the gathers to the back and secure them there with a few backstitches. But don't cut the threads just yet: stab stitch (see page 88) around the edge of the gathered circle, taking the needle up and down in a gather trough every ¾in (2cm) or so, to hold the gathered edge flat against the bag. This isn't vital, especially on small yo-yos, but it does help larger ones to sit neatly.

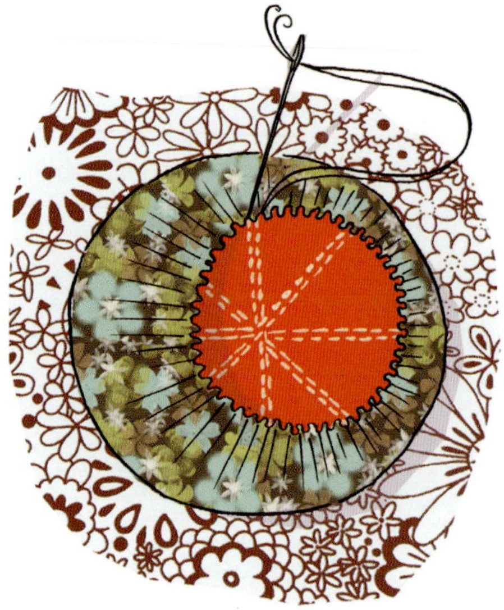

9 I sewed buttons into the center of my yo-yos using fly stitch: bring the needle up through one buttonhole and down through another, but don't pull the thread tight. Bring the needle up beyond the edge of the button, between the positions of the two holes, and take it through the loop of thread. Pull the thread taut, then make a short straight stitch to finish the fly stitch (see also page 88). I used four-hole buttons and made four fly stitches, so that each button is held down by a stitched star. I also sewed some orange buttons to the centers of some of the printed flowers on the bag fabric.

To make up the bag

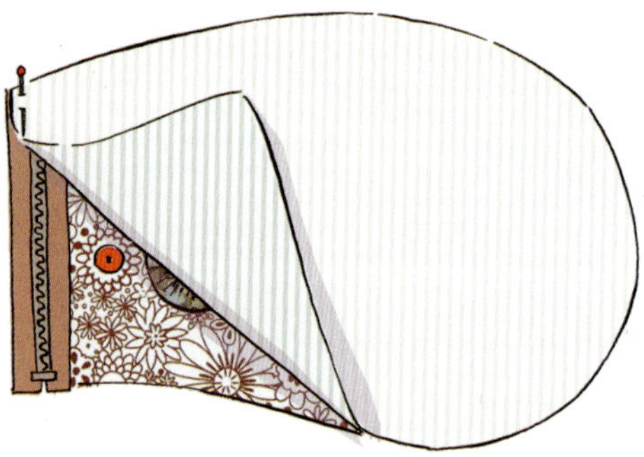

10 Bits of the next few steps might seem complicated, but take it slowly and all will be well. Lay the decorated bag front piece face up, and lay the zipper face down on top of it, so that all of the zipper is lying on the fabric with the edge of one tape against the top edge of the fabric. Lay a lining piece face down on top, matching the edges to the front bag piece. Pin and then baste the pieces together along the upper zipper tape.

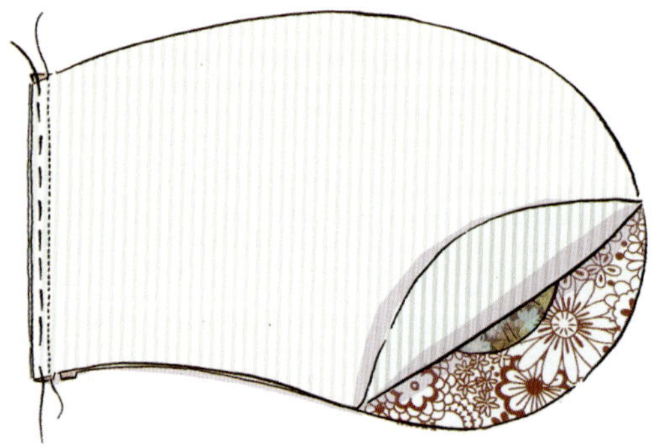

11 Fit a zipper foot to the sewing machine and sew along the basted tape. You can sew as near to the teeth as you want: I like the exposed zipper look, so I sewed quite close to the outer edge of the tape.

12 Fold the lining and main fabric wrong sides together, so that the zipper sticks out, as shown. Press the seam flat.

13 Open the lining and main fabric out again and zigzag along the seam allowance (for extra strength). Then fold the seam allowance flat against the lining, and sew a line of straight stitch about ⅛in (3mm) below the seam line, understitching the lining to the seam allowance. This will help stop the lining getting caught in the zipper when you open the bag. Fold the lining and main fabric right sides together again, and give the seam another quick press.

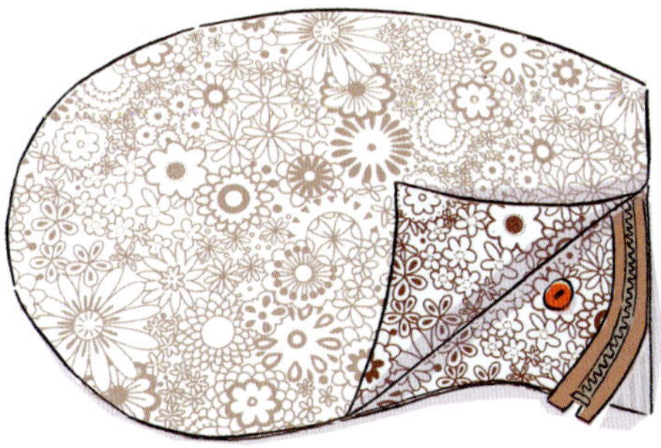

14 To sew the bag back and lining to the other zipper tape, first lay the back lining flat and face up. Lay the front bag and lining (treat them as one piece), face up on top, positioning the free edge of the zipper tape against the top edge of the back lining. Then lay the bag back on top, matching the edges to the back lining. Pin and then baste the pieces together along the free zipper tape. Follow Steps 11–13 to sew the fabric pieces to the zipper.

15 When you open the bag pieces out, it should look like a (rather peculiar) butterfly, with the zipper as its body. Undo the zipper halfway; this is vital.

16 Fold the bag pieces together, linings facing out. Using sewing thread, whip stitch (see page 87) the ends of the tapes together, at each end of the zipper.

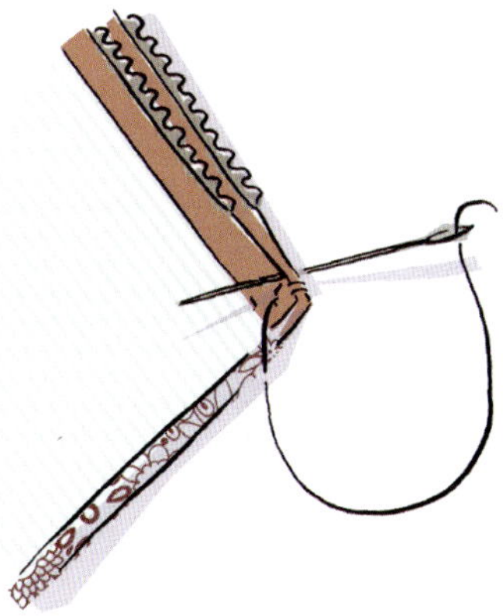

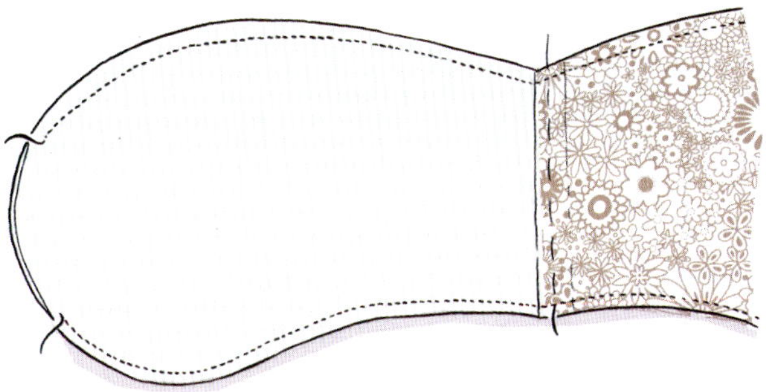

17 Open the bag out so that the linings are right sides together, as are the main pieces: the zipper will be invisible. Pin the layers together right around the edges. Take time to make sure the zipper tapes are neatly folded down toward the lining; if they are a bit unruly it's worth basting them. Starting near the bottom of the lining, sew right around the edge of the whole shape, leaving a 4in (10cm) gap in the lining.

18 Reach in through the gap in the lining and carefully pull the main bag through the half-opened zipper (now you see why it was vital!), and carry on pulling it right through the gap in the lining. Continue pulling until the lining is right side out, too. Press the seams flat, pressing under the seam allowances across the gap in the lining, then ladder stitch (see page 88) the gap closed. Tuck the lining inside the bag and you're done.

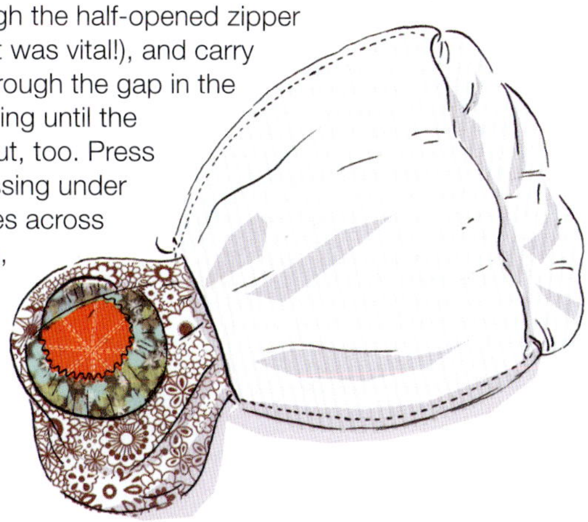

Safe storage belt

My regulation school summer dresses were pink-and-white striped sacks with narrow collars, zipped-up fronts, and too-short sleeves: everyone, absolutely everyone, looked terrible in them. The amount of customizing that could be done was severely curtailed by strict uniform regulations, but one accessory that was permitted was a purse belt, though it did have to be maroon. At least it gave the sack a bit of shape. And you had somewhere to keep your candy money. And when I left school I kept the belt and wore it to festivals to keep cash safe. And when the belt fell apart, I kept the clasp, and that is the clasp on this belt. So it is worth hoarding the odd thing or two... See below for tips on altering this belt design to suit your own clasp or buckle.

YOU'RE GOING TO NEED...

- Fabric and medium-weight fusible interfacing (see Customizing the Belt Design, below)
- Fabric scissors
- Iron and ironing board
- 6in (15cm) zipper
- Pins
- Hand-sewing needle
- Basting thread: I always use ordinary sewing thread in a contrast color
- Sewing threads to match fabrics
- Sewing machine
- Buckle or clasp (see Customizing The Belt Design, below)
- Masking tape
- Eyelets to fit buckle tongue (if you are using a buckle rather than a clasp)

CUSTOMIZING THE BELT DESIGN

The width of the belt is determined by the width of the part of the clasp or buckle that the fabric is attached to (see Step 7). So a narrow clasp will only give you a very skinny pocket. For a clasp, you need two strips of fabric and one of medium-weight fusible interfacing that measure the required width plus ¾in (2cm), by your waist measurement plus 4in (10cm). I made my strips longer than this as my original purse belt had an adjustable slider and I wanted to use it on this belt, too. If you're using a buckle, then the same width is needed, but you need extra length to thread through the buckle: experiment with your buckle and a strip of paper to see how much fabric you need.

1 Iron the interfacing onto the back of one of the fabric strips; this will be the outer side of the belt. Press under a ⅜-in (1-cm) hem along one long edge of each belt piece.

2 Position the zipper face down on the hem of the interfaced fabric, with the teeth of one tape aligned with the folded edge of the hem. If you are right-handed (as I am), then you want the zipper pull about 4in (10cm) from the right-hand end of the belt: the same distance from the left-hand end if you are left-handed. (I had to put the strip around my waist, right side out and folded hem uppermost, to work out where my zipper should go: I recommend the same procedure for safety.) Pin and then baste the tape in position.

3 Making sure the ends of both strips are aligned, repeat the process to baste the folded edge of the other strip to the other zipper tape.

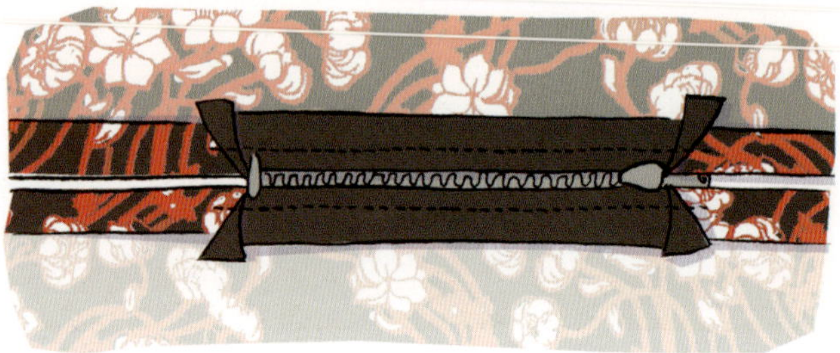

4 Fold the ends of the tapes away from the zipper teeth, as shown. Machine-sew close to the teeth on each side, sewing over the folded tapes, to sew the zipper in place.

5 Fold the two fabric strips right sides together. Taking ⅜-in (1-cm) seam allowances, and reversing at each end, sew along the pressed fold at the top from either end of the zipper to the ends of the strips. Sew as close to the ends of the zipper as you can, so that there won't be any holes in your pocket. Then sew right along the bottom edge.

6 Turn the belt right side out through one of the open short ends and press it flat. Tuck in ⅜in (1cm) at each short end and press.

7 Slip one short end through one half of the clasp and sew it to the inside layer of the belt. Repeat on the other end with the other half of the clasp. It you are using a buckle, attach it to one end of the belt in this way, and follow the instructions of the eyelet kit to fit eyelets into the other end of the belt.

8 To make the pocket, stick strips of masking tape across the belt just beyond either end of the zipper. Sew along these guidelines, reversing at each end to secure the stitching.

Damp-proof picnic mat

There are only three not-lovely things about camping, and a damp derrière is one of them. (Since you ask, small flying things that bite and erratic facilities are the others.) Thankfully, damp unmentionables are easily averted with a practical but also deeply gorgeous mat. The waterproof backing is topped with patchwork: I've included some crochet granny squares in my version, but yours can be just as perfect made entirely from fabric.

YOU'RE GOING TO NEED...

- Piece of oilcloth (or similar plastic-backed fabric), the size you want the mat to be: mine is 42 x 30in (110 x 80cm)
- Small pieces of medium-weight fabrics: I used corduroy and wool woven fabrics, plus a bit of an old sweater (the orange cabled patch), and some crochet granny squares (see Crochet: Granny Squares on page 89, to make your own)
- Enough 2-in (5-cm) wide cotton tape to go right around your mat, plus 8in (20cm) for mitering corners and neatening the ends (see also Dye It on page 43)
- Fabric scissors
- Iron and ironing board
- Pins
- Sewing threads to match fabrics
- Sewing machine

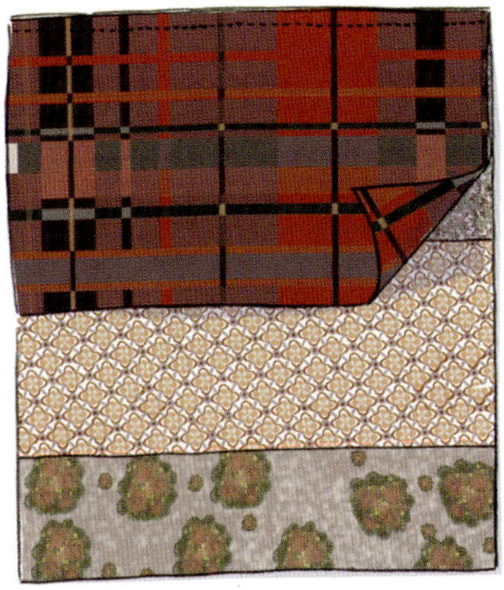

1 The way to make up the patchwork top is to sew together pieces into strips and then join these in rows. So, the patches in each strip need to be the same width, but can be different lengths. Stagger the horizontal seams in adjacent strips to reduce bulk. Cut two patches to the same width and pin them right sides together. Sew the seam taking a ⅜-in (1-cm) seam allowance, and press the seam open. Repeat to make a strip of patches.

2 If you are incorporating granny squares into your mat, then they will determine the width of the strips they are in. The pattern (see page 89) has an extra round of single (double) crochet around the edge, and this acts as a seam allowance. I found it easiest to press under the seam allowances of fabric patches to be joined to crochet squares, then I could see to position the edge of the fabric in the right place on the crochet and pin the pieces together. Open the seam allowances out and sew the seam along the pressed line.

3 If you pin and sew carefully, the seam will be very neat on the crochet squares as well as the fabric. Avoid having a crochet square on any edges of the mat, as the binding (see Step 6) will intrude into the pattern.

4 Sew the strips together to make the patchwork mat top. When you are sewing, you might find it easiest to have strips with crochet squares uppermost, then you can see to sew across them in the right place.

5 Lay the patchwork mat top on the waterproof backing, wrong sides together. Smooth the top flat and pin the layers together close to the edge: don't put pins elsewhere in the mat or its waterproofness will be compromised and a damp derrière will creep in. Trim any excess fabric from the patchwork to fit the backing, then sew right around the edge, ¼in (6mm) in, to hold the layers together.

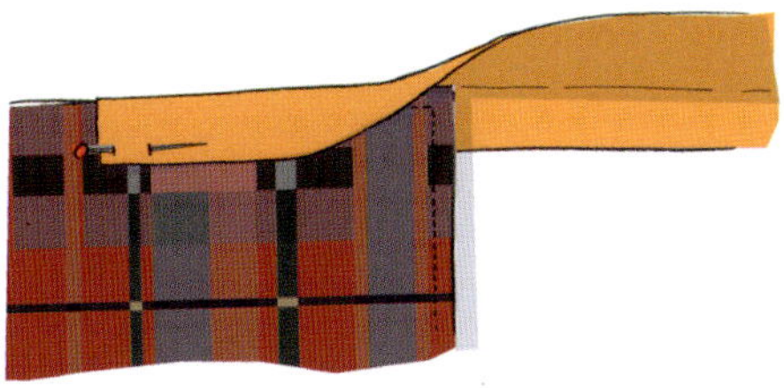

6 Press the cotton tape in half lengthwise. Starting a short distance before one corner, fold the tape over the edge of the mat and pin in place to the corner.

7 Stitching about ¼in (6mm) from the edge, sew up to the corner, reversing at the start and end of the stitching to secure it.

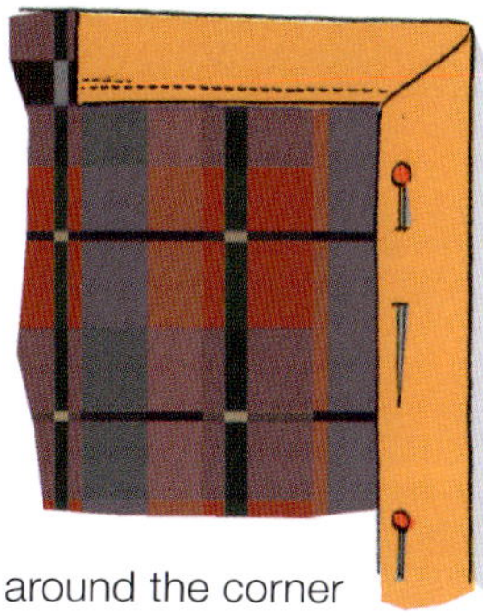

8 Fold the tape around the corner to make a neat miter. Pin and then sew the tape in place right along to the next corner. Repeat at every corner to bind the edges of the whole mat.

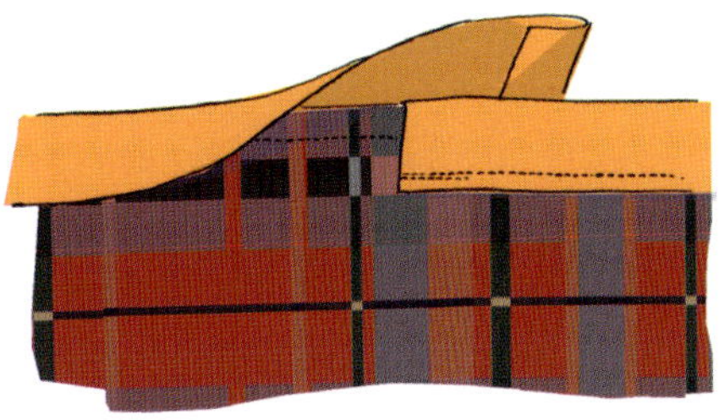

9 Before sewing the last edge, fold ⅜in (1cm) of the end of the tape under, trimming off any excess as needed, and lap it over the starting point. Pin in place, then sew the tape, sewing right over the folded end.

DYE IT

I could only find the cotton tape I wanted in cream or black, so I bought cream and dyed it bright orange to go with my mat. But it did shrink a bit... So if you are going to custom-dye tape, buy a yard (meter) more than you need (it won't shrink quite that much, but the tape isn't expensive, and better safe than sorry). While I was dyeing my tape I ombre-dyed a piece of corduroy; you can see it in the mat. I washed the fabric and while it was damp, dunked one end into the dye batch and clothes-pinned the other end to the faucet. I left it for an hour, and while the dye didn't creep very far up the fabric, the effect was good.

Washbag

I made this as a weekend washbag; it's perfect for the travel-sized lotions and potions I take with me when I'm only away for a couple of days. Choose cotton fabrics so that the bag is washable if anything leaks.

YOU'RE GOING TO NEED...

- Templates on pages 90–91
- One piece of fabric measuring 12 x 8in (30 x 20cm), one piece measuring 13 x 6in (33 x 15cm), and one piece measuring 9 x 3in (23 x 8cm): I used quilting cottons
- 8-in (20-cm) zipper
- Paper for templates
- Paper scissors and fabric scissors
- Tape measure
- Iron and ironing board
- Pins
- Sewing threads to match fabrics
- Sewing machine with zipper foot
- Hand-sewing needle

1 Using the templates on pages 90–91, cut out one back from the largest piece of fabric, one bottom front from the middle-sized piece, and one top front from the smallest piece.

2 Press under a ⅜-in (1-cm) hem across the top straight edge of the bottom front piece, then open it flat again. Make a series of small pleats in the top edge, pleating the fabric until the length of that edge matches the length of the bottom edge of the top front. You can make the pleats symmetrical or not, as you choose: I made random pleats. Set the sewing machine to a small zigzag stitch and sew across the pleats within the hem to hold them in place.

3 Position one of the zipper tapes right side down on the right side of the pleated hem, so that the endstop is ⅝in (1.5cm) from the edge and the pressed edge of the hem is against the zipper teeth. Baste (tack) the tape in place. Using a zipper foot, sew the tape in place, sewing very close to the teeth.

4 In the same way as in Step 3, and taking a ⅜-in (1-cm) seam allowance, baste and then sew the other zipper tape to the bottom edge of the top front. Neaten the seam allowances by trimming them to the width of the tapes and then zigzagging the tape to the fabric.

5 Oversew the ends of the zipper tapes together. Undo the zipper halfway.

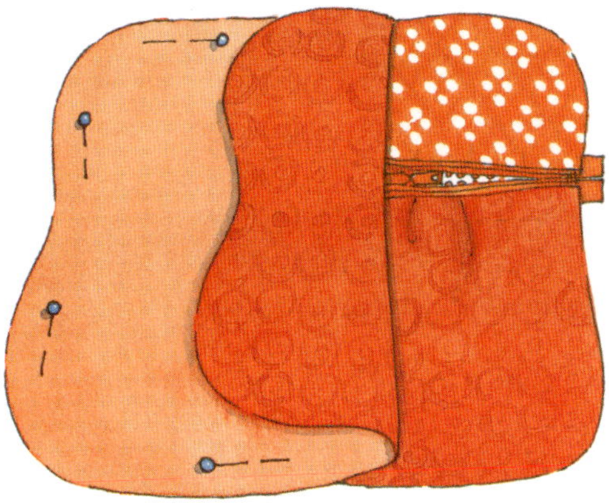

6 Pin the front and back right sides together, matching the raw edges and easing the pieces to fit as needed. Taking a ⅜-in (1-cm) seam allowance, sew all around the edges. Zigzag and trim the seam allowances, then turn the bag right side out through the zipper. Press the seams flat.

Tote bag

Strong, secure, and seriously stylish, this is the perfect tote bag. The drawstring top pulls tight over your shopping to keep everything safe. For a quick-and-easy tote, you can simply leave out the lining and drawstring sections and just hem the top edge of the bag.

YOU'RE GOING TO NEED...

- Fabric and cord: see How Much Fabric?, right
- Tassel or charm, if required
- Tape measure
- Fabric scissors
- Iron and ironing board
- Pins
- Pinking shears
- Sewing threads to match fabrics
- Sewing machine
- Fading fabric marker
- Hand-sewing needle

HOW MUCH FABRIC?

You can make a tote bag almost any size you want. You'll need:

- Two pieces of medium- to heavy-weight outer fabric measuring the width of the bag plus 1¼in (3cm), by the length of the bag plus 1¼in (3cm)
- Two pieces of light- to medium-weight lining fabric measuring the width of the bag plus 1¼in (3cm), by the length of the bag plus 1¼in (3cm)
- Two pieces of light- to medium-weight fabric for the drawstring top measuring the width of the bag plus 1¼in (3cm), by one-third of the length of the bag plus 2in (5cm)
- Two pieces of medium- to heavy-weight handle fabric measuring twice the finished width plus 1¼in (3cm), by the length plus 1¼in (3cm)
- Two lengths of ribbon or cord twice the width of the bag plus 6in (15cm): I used suede ribbon

1 Right sides together and taking a ⅝-in (1.5-cm) seam allowance, sew the two outer pieces together around three sides, leaving the short top edge open. Sew the lining in the same way, but leave a 4-in (10-cm) gap in the middle of the short bottom edge. At the top open edge, press about 1in (2.5cm) of the seams open. Turn the outer piece right side out, but leave the lining wrong side out.

2 Pin the drawstring pieces right sides together. Starting at the top edge and taking a ⅝-in (1.5-cm) seam allowance, sew 1⅜in (3.5cm) of one side seam, then reverse to secure the stitches. Leave a ⅜-in (1-cm) gap, then sew the rest of the seam, reversing at each end. Sew the other side seam in the same way, then press both seams open and trim the seam allowances with pinking shears.

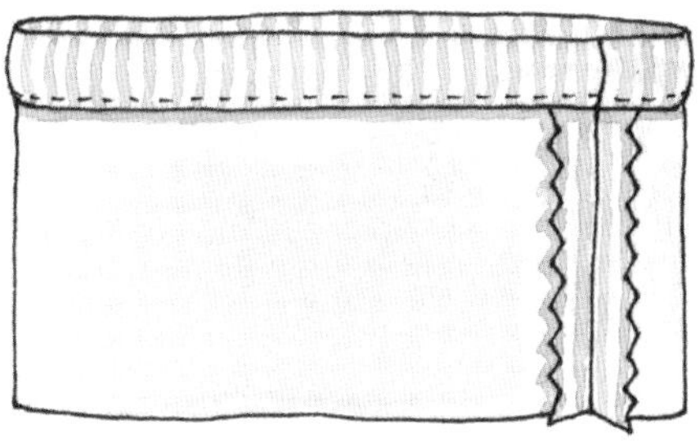

3 Press under a ⅜-in (1-cm) then a ¾-in (2-cm) hem around the top edge of the drawstring piece. Sew the hem very close to the bottom edge to make a channel for the drawstring. The gaps in the side seam should now be in the middle of the hem on the right side of the piece.

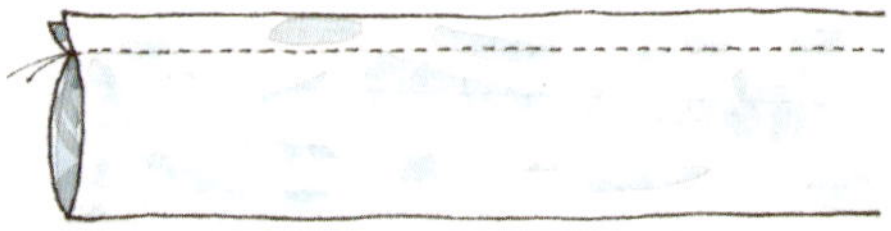

4 Right side in, fold a handle strip in half lengthwise. Taking a ⅝-in (1.5-cm) seam allowance, sew the seam. Press the seam open, then turn the handle right side out (see page 86). Roll the seam to the center back and press the handle flat. Repeat for the other handle strip.

5 Seam uppermost, pin and then zigzag stitch a handle to the top edge of the right side of the front and back of the bag. Make sure that the handles aren't twisted before you sew them on.

6 Right sides together, slip the drawstring section over the top of the outer bag, matching the side seams and the raw bottom edge of the drawstring section with the raw top edge of the bag.

7 Next, slip the outer bag/drawstring pieces into the inside-out lining, matching the side seams and the raw top edge of the lining with the already matched raw edges of the outer and drawstring pieces. Pin all the layers together around the matched raw edges, then, taking a ⅝-in (1.5-cm) seam allowance, sew right around the top edge.

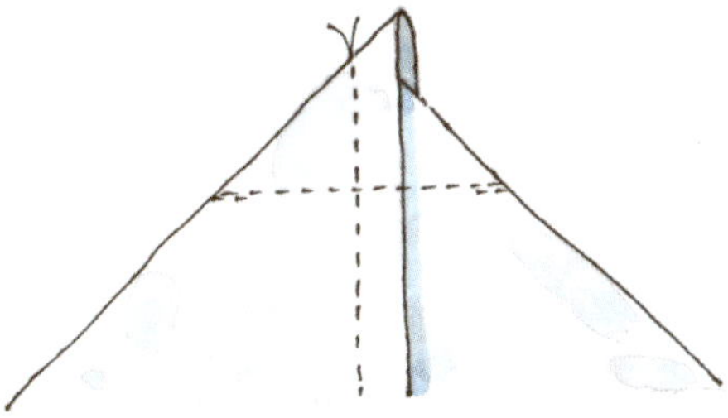

8 Pull the outer bag up out of the lining, and, with both layers inside out, make the square corners. Fold an outer-bag corner flat, so that the bottom seam aligns with a side seam, and pin the seams together through all the layers. Measure down the seam 2in (5cm) from the point, and draw a line across the corner, at right angles to the seam, as shown. Machine-sew along this line, reversing at both ends to secure the stitching. Sew the other corner the same way, making sure that the seam allowance is lying to the same side.

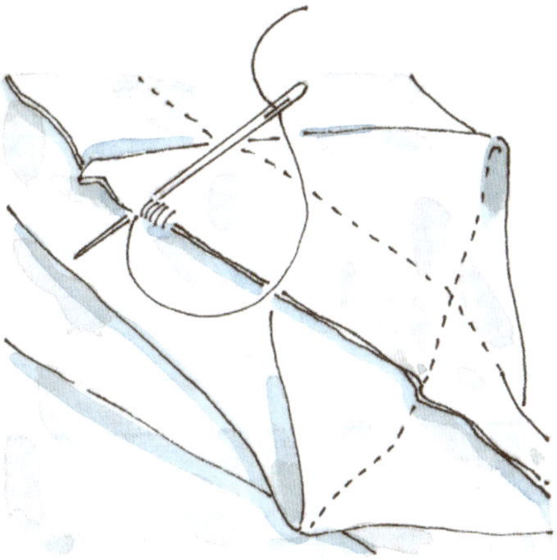

9 At the sewn line, fold each corner over toward the bottom of the bag and hand sew the point to the seam allowance of the bottom seam. Repeat Steps 8 and 9 on the corners of the lining.

10 Turn the whole bag out through the gap in the lining, pulling the outer bag through, then continuing to pull until the lining is right side out, too. Press under the seam allowances across the gap in the lining, then sew the gap closed; either machine-sew very close to the edge, as I have, or use ladder stitch (see page 88). Tuck the lining down inside the bag and press the seam around the top edge flat.

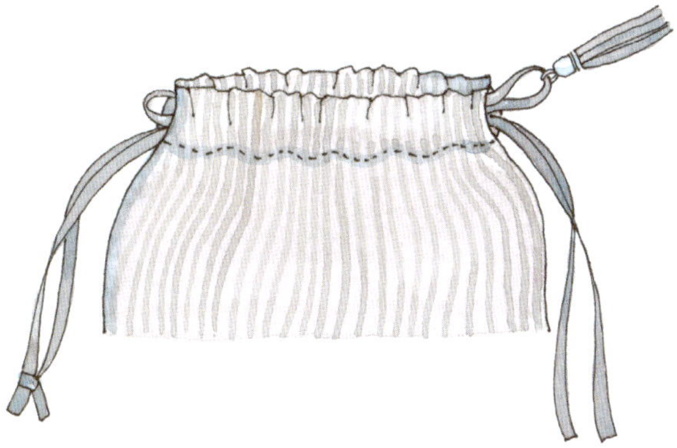

11 Thread the ribbon through one side of the channel in the drawstring section, from one gap in the side seam to the other gap. Thread on a tassel or charm, if you want, then thread the ribbon through the other side of the channel to come out through the first gap again. Knot the ends of the ribbon together. Repeat the process with the second length of ribbon, but starting at the opposite gap to the first ribbon.

Outdoor bunting

There's an art, a skill, a science… a something to camping in style. A guru of good-looking camping always, but always, has bunting up around their tent and gazebo. The bunting I've made here can be simplified if you're going away tomorrow—see **Super-simple bunting**—but the full version doesn't take long and will give you years of gleeful glamping.

YOU'RE GOING TO NEED…

- Selection of lightweight cotton fabrics: see Shapes and Sizes, below
- Iron and ironing board
- Rotary cutter, ruler, and cutting mat, or fabric scissors
- Pins
- Sewing threads to match fabrics
- Sewing machine
- Point turner or chopstick
- ⅝-in (1.5-cm) wide bias binding the length you want the bunting to be, plus 8in (20cm): see Shapes and Sizes, below
- Pom-pom trim (optional)
- Scraps of ribbon (optional)

SHAPES AND SIZES

This is a great stash buster project; fabric pieces as small as 6in (15cm) square will make good pennants. And because the triangles are different sizes, you can use up oddly shaped leftovers from other projects.

I used a single color palette, with checks, stripes, spots, and star patterns, but that's just my taste. My bunting is approximately 4yd (3.75m) long finished length, and has 12 pennants on it.

1 Cut out half the number of pennants you want, the size and precise shape can be determined by the fabrics you have available. I cut 12 pennants: the smallest is 5¾in (14.5cm) wide and 7in (17.5cm) from top to tip, and the largest is 9½in (24cm) wide and 9in (23cm) from top to tip. I had gingham fabrics with three sizes of squares, so I cut all my first batch of pennants from these as that was the easiest way of making the patterns work neatly. For **super-simple bunting**, cut out the pieces using pinking shears or a rotary cutter with a pinking blade.

2 Right sides together, pin the cut out pennants to other pieces of fabric. For **super-simple bunting**, skip this step and the next three steps and go straight to Step 6.

3 Taking ⅜-in (1-cm) seam allowances, machine sew the pennants to the fabric. Sew down one sloping side, lift the presser foot and pivot the fabric then make a couple of stitches straight across the pennant, then pivot the fabric again to sew up the other sloping side. This will help you make the neatest points. Leave the top straight edge unstitched.

4 Cut the pennants out, at the same time trimming the seam allowances to about ¼in (6mm) and cutting off the excess fabric at the point. A rotary cutter and ruler offer the quickest and easiest method of doing this.

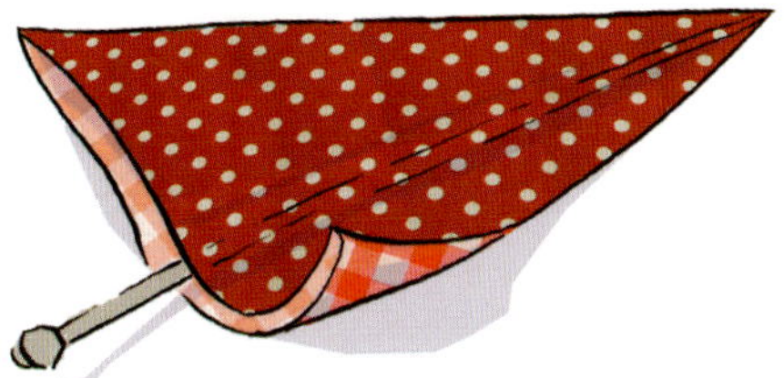

5 Turn the pennants right side out, pushing out the point with a point turner or a knitting needle or chopstick. Press the pennants flat.

6 Iron the bias binding in half lengthwise. Lay it out flat (you'll probably need to do this on the floor) and space the pennants out along it. I spaced mine irregularly, making sure that adjacent pennants were different shapes, and that the different fabric patterns were evenly distributed. When you are happy with the arrangement, take a digital photo to refer back to. Stack the flags in a pile in the order in which you'll sew them to the binding (see Step 10).

7 The pom-poms are very optional, but do add an extra jaunty note to the bunting. Cut individual pom-poms off a length of pom-pom trim, pulling out the linking cord as far as possible on each pom-pom before cutting it off: don't worry if the separate pom-poms end up with tails of different lengths, they can just hang at different heights. For **super-simple bunting**, skip this bit.

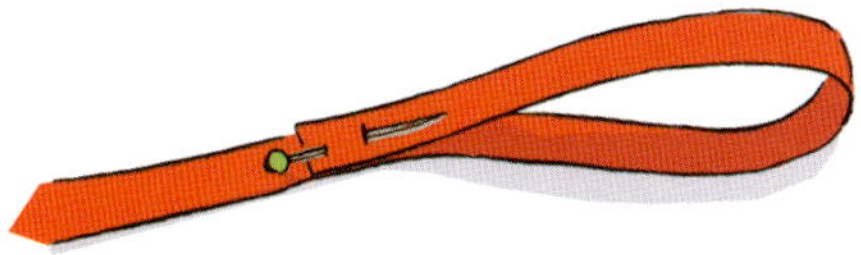

8 Fold over 2in (5cm) at one end of the binding to make a loop (to hang the bunting by) and pin it in place.

9 Set the sewing machine to a medium zigzag stitch. Put the pinned end of the loop under the needle, making sure the open edge of the binding is facing to the left. Start zigzag stitching along the binding, sewing the loop in place, then reversing to secure the stitching and strengthen the loop. Zigzag along a short length then slip the tails of a pom-pom into the folded binding and zigzag over them. For **super-simple bunting**, don't include the pom-poms.

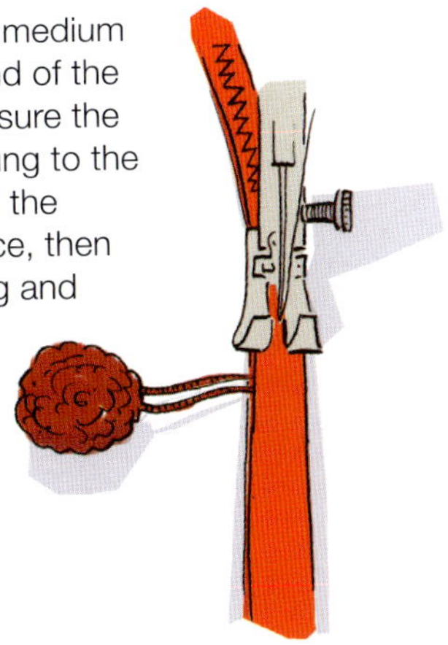

10 Zigzag another short distance, then, referring back to your photo (or just winging it a bit, as I did), slip in the raw edges of the first pennant in your stack and zigzag over that. Continue in this way (I did alternate pom-poms and pennants) until you have about 6–8in (15–20cm) of binding left to sew. Fold over the last 2in (5cm) to make a loop and sew up to it, sewing down the end then reversing to secure the stitching and strengthen the loop.

11 For final (optional) perkiness, knot a scrap of ribbon around the binding between the tails of each pom-pom. For **super-simple bunting**, skip this bit (obviously).

CHAPTER 3
To Wear

Pretty practical apron

An apron is a cooking necessity (especially if you are a cook as enthusiastic but messy as I am), but to be a hostess with the mostest, it needs to be lovely as well as capacious; so that you can pop in and out of the kitchen and join in the party without constantly taking your apron off, forgetting to put it back on again, and spilling cooking ingredients down your front. I like a longish apron as I wear a lot of long skirts, but you can easily adapt this pattern to suit both the length you like and your waist size—see Size Matters, below, and the **change this** notes in the steps.

YOU'RE GOING TO NEED...

- 28in (70cm) of each of jumbo and super-jumbo rick rack: see Suppliers, page 95
- For the skirt: one piece of main fabric measuring 28 x 14in (70 x 35cm); one piece measuring 28 x 7in (70 x 18cm); and one piece of contrast fabric measuring 28 x 3in (70 x 8cm): I used quilting cottons
- For the waistband: one piece of contrast fabric measuring the width of the finished top of the apron (see Step 7) plus 1¼in (3cm) by 6in (15cm), and one piece of fusible interfacing measuring the same width by 3in (7.5cm) deep
- For the ties: two pieces of contrast fabric measuring about 23½in (60cm) or the length required, by 6in (15cm)
- 1in (2.5cm) bias binding, the length of the finished bottom of the apron plus ¾in (2cm): mine measured 22in (56cm)
- Sewing threads to match fabrics and rick rack
- Hand-sewing needle
- Pins
- Sewing machine
- Fabric scissors
- Iron and ironing board

SIZE MATTERS

The instructions will give you an apron measuring approximately 28in (70cm) long, and 15in (38cm) across the top, with ties 23½in (60cm) long. To increase the width a small amount you can either reduce the depth of the pleats (see Step 6) or cut wider main fabric panels. To increase the width by more than an inch (2.5cm) or so, cut wider main fabric panels, but leave the contrast strip the same width.

1 Turn under and stitch down a small hem at one end of each piece of rick rack. Rick rack does tend to fray rather horribly, so you might find some fray-check useful here.

2 Right sides together, lay the jumbo rick rack along the left-hand long edge of the large piece of main fabric, with the turned under end ⅜in (1cm) up from a short raw edge. Position the rick rack so that when a ⅝in (1.5cm) seam is sewn along the long edge, the seam will run along the middle of the rick rack: shown here by the dashed line. Pin the rick rack in place along the upper edge.

3 Lay the contrast strip for the skirt right side down over the rick rack, matching the raw edges with the raw edges of the main piece. Pin the layers together, making sure you pin through the rick rack, then take out the pins inserted in Step 2. Sew the seam taking a ⅝-in (1.5-cm) seam allowance. Finish the raw seam allowances by zigzag stitching them and the rick rack together.

4 Press the seam flat on the right side, pressing the rick rack toward the contrast strip, and on the wrong side pressing the rick rack and both seam allowances toward the main fabric.

5 Repeat Steps 2–4 with the super-jumbo rick rack, pinning it right sides together to the raw edge of the contrast strip, then pinning the smaller piece of main fabric over it. Press the rick rack and seam allowances in the same direction as the first piece. On the right side, topstitch ⅛in (3mm) from the rick rack seams to hold the seam allowances flat.

6 Pleat the top edge of the apron. I made three pleats, each over 2¼in (6cm) of fabric, placing one pleat 2½in (6.5cm) in from each edge and another one in the larger main fabric, 1½in (4cm) from the first pleat. You can **change this** arrangement to suit, but keep the pleats at least 1¼in (3cm) from the long edges, and don't put a pleat into the contrast strip (it'll get muddled up in the rick rack seams and be very bulky). On the right side, topstitch a short way down the pleats to hold them in place: I topstitched about 4in (10cm), but you can **change this** by stitching a shorter amount for a fuller apron. At this stage my apron was 16½in (42cm) wide across the top edge.

7 Turn under and sew a double ⅜-in (1-cm) hem along each long edge. This made the top edge of my apron a finished width of 15in (38cm).

8 Iron the fusible interfacing onto the back of half of the waistband fabric, as shown. Right sides together, pin one tie piece to each end of the waistband. Taking ⅝-in (1.5-cm) seam allowances, sew the pieces together. Press the seam allowances open.

9 Right sides together, pin the interfaced edge of the waistband to the top of the skirt, matching the waistband side seams to the edges of the skirt. Sew the pieces together, taking a ⅜-in (1-cm) seam allowance.

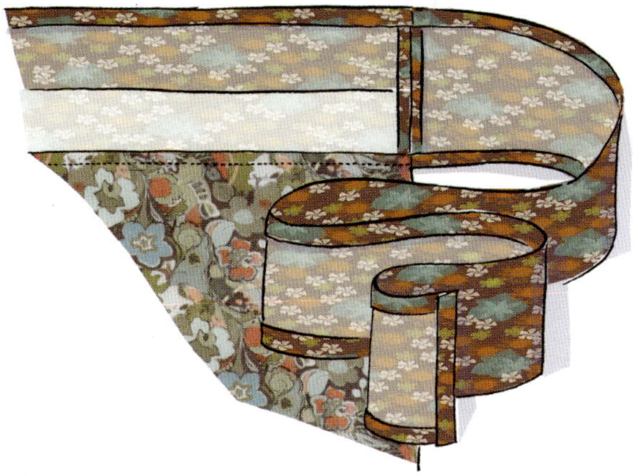

10 Open the pieces out and press the seam flat, pressing the seam allowance toward the waistband. Press under ⅜-in (1-cm) hems around all the other edges of the waistband/tie piece.

11 Fold the piece in half along the interfacing and matching the edges of the ties exactly, and sew all around.

12 Open out one folded edge of the bias binding and, right sides together, pin it to the bottom edge of the apron, matching the edge of the binding to the edge of the apron as shown, and so that ⅜in (1cm) protrudes at either side. Sew along the fold in the binding.

13 Fold in the free ends of the binding and press. Then fold the binding over to the wrong side of the apron, folding over just a little of the fabric as well, as shown. Sew along the top edge of the binding to finish the hem. I stopped and started sewing either side of the rick rack, but that isn't strictly necessary.

Pearly Peter Pan collar

Little House on the Prairie meets a London Pearly Queen: wear it over a sweater or boat-neck top as a collar, or with a sundress as a festival necklace (it's quick to make, so if it ends up covered in mud, you can just wash it, or cut off the buttons and start again). Alternatively, make your version from black velvet with vintage jet and silver buttons for gothic bling, or go for a button-box-raid look with a heavy sprinkling of buttons of all shapes, sizes, and colors on a collar of candy-stripe cotton, or... There are as many options as there are buttons and fabrics: that's a lot of options.

YOU'RE GOING TO NEED...

- Collar template on page 92
- Sheet of newspaper
- Paper scissors and fabric scissors
- Two pieces of fabric and one piece of medium-weight fusible interfacing, each measuring 13 x 20½in (33 x 52cm): I used linen fabric
- Iron and ironing board
- Pins
- 1yd (1m) of ⅝-in (1.5-mm) wide tape or ribbon: I used linen tape
- Basting thread and sewing thread to match fabric and trim
- Hand-sewing needle
- Sewing machine
- 37½in (95cm) of narrow trim: I used a small daisy trim
- Selection of buttons: I used vintage mother-of-pearl
- Six-strand embroidery floss
- Embroidery needle

1 Enlarge the template by 200 percent. To make a muslin, fold the newspaper in half, place the center back of the template on the fold and cut out a paper collar. Cut off ⅜in (1cm) all around (you don't have to measure this perfectly, a rough cut will do). Try on this paper muslin to make sure the collar will be the right size for you. If need be, adjust the paper muslin to fit and make a bespoke pattern, remembering to add the seam allowances back on. Cut out two fabric collars and one from interfacing. Iron the interfacing onto one fabric piece, then trim off ⅛in (3mm) all around the outer edge; this piece will be the undercollar.

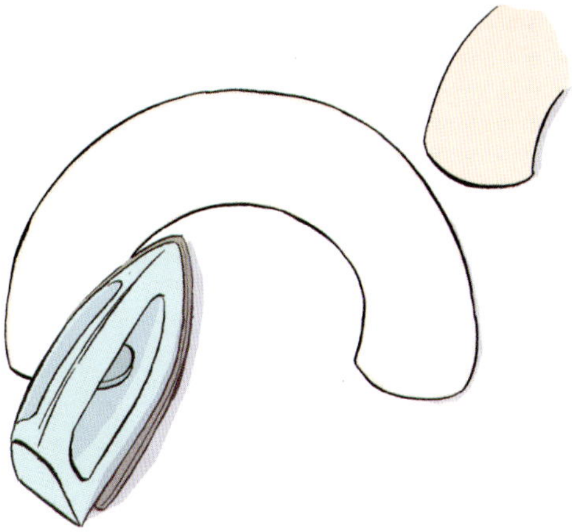

2 Cut the tape in half. Pin one end of each half to the front edge of the right side of the undercollar, ½in (12mm) from the inside neck edge, as shown. Make sure the ends of the tapes are square to the edges of the collar, then baste them in place.

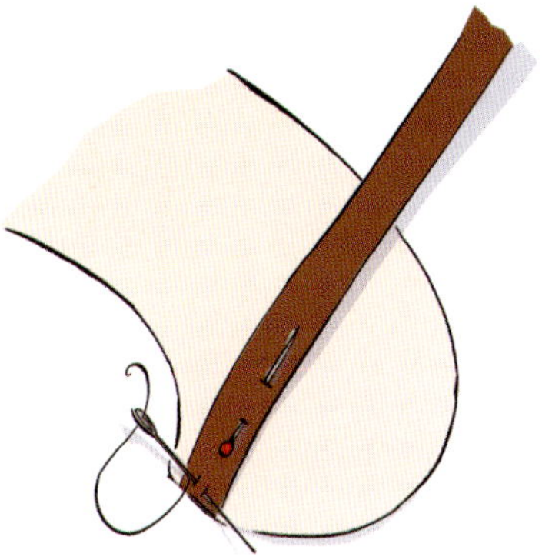

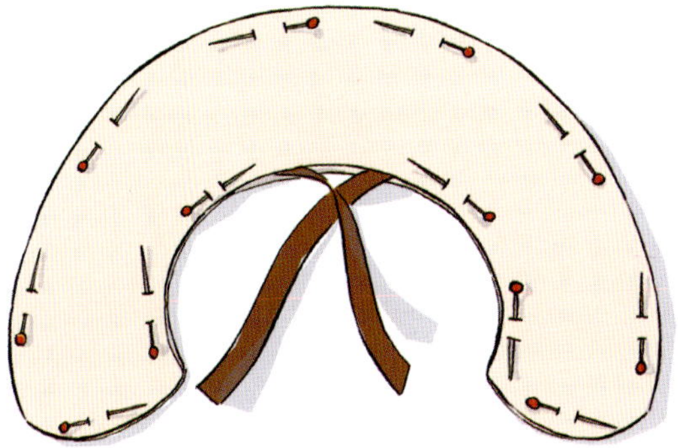

3 Lay the other fabric piece right-side down on top of the undercollar and pin the pieces together around the edges. Leave a 4in (10cm) gap in the center back neck, and pull the ends of the tape through the gap so that you can see them.

4 Sew around the pinned edges, taking a ⅜-in (1-cm) seam allowance, and pivoting at the neck-edge corners. Be very careful not to catch the tapes in the stitching. Clip notches in the seam allowances, clipping to within ⅛in (3mm) of the line of stitching (see page 86). Make notches close together on tightly curved or short sections, and space them more widely on gentle, longer curves.

5 Turn the collar right side out through the gap. Press the seams, rolling them to the undercollar side as you go, and press under the seam allowances across the gap. Ladder stitch (see page 88) the gap closed.

6 Hand-sew the trim around the edge of the collar. Make tiny stitches in matching thread through the trim, and through the upper layer only of the collar, to sew it on as invisibly as possible.

7 Arrange buttons on each end of the collar (or all around it if you prefer) and take digital photos. Sew on the buttons one at a time, using your photos as guides. Use one, two, or three strands of six-strand floss, as appropriate for the size of the button. You can use decorative stitches, such as fly stitch: bring the needle and floss out through one hole in the button and down through another, leaving a loose loop of floss. Then bring the needle up though the fabric at the edge of the button, and through the loop of floss. Make a short straight stitch to anchor the loop and complete the fly stitch (see also page 88). Four fly stitches on a four-hole button will make a star; two stitches on a two-hole button will make a diamond.

8 Or you can use chain stitch: bring the needle and floss out through one hole in the button and down through the same hole, leaving a loose loop of floss. Then bring the needle up through the fabric at the edge of the button, and through the loop of floss. Make a short straight stitch to anchor the loop and complete the chain stitch (see also page 87). You can work a line of three chain stitches across a two-hole button (the middle stitch will span the holes). You can also work straight stitches in squares or crosses on four-hole buttons.

Big bow hairband

Here's a perky hair bow that you can make from just a few scraps of fabric, to match a dress you've made maybe? And it's not just a project for little girls; big girls look good with bows, too. Though if you aren't the bow type, you can just stop at Step 4 and make a simple, but chic, hairband.

YOU'RE GOING TO NEED...

- For the band: strip of fabric and strip of lightweight fusible interfacing, each measuring 3in (8cm) shorter than the circumference of your head where you want the band to sit, by 4¾in (12cm)
- 4in (10cm) of 1¼-in (3-cm) wide elastic
- For the bow: two pieces of fabric measuring 9½ x 8in (24 x 20cm) and one piece measuring 3½ x 2¾in (9 x 7cm)
- Fabric scissors
- Iron and ironing board
- Pins
- Sewing threads to match fabrics
- Sewing machine
- Hand-sewing needle

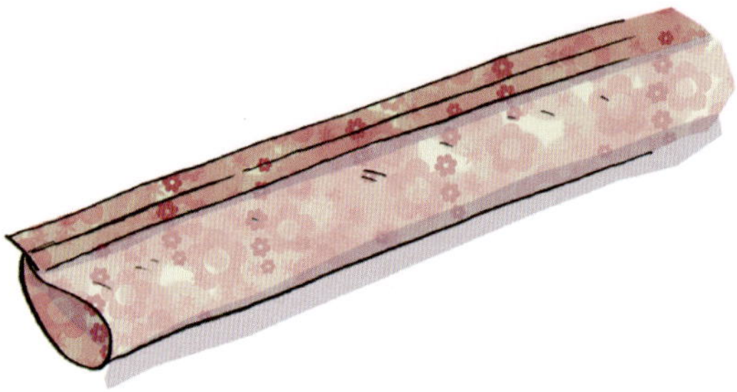

1 Iron the interfacing onto the back of the band piece of fabric. Right side in, fold the fabric in half lengthwise and, taking a ⅜-in (1-cm) seam allowance, sew the long seam. Fold back one seam allowance and press open, without pressing a fold in the tube of fabric.

2 Turn the tube right side out. Roll the seam to center back and press the tube flat. Tuck in ⅜in (1cm) at each end and press flat.

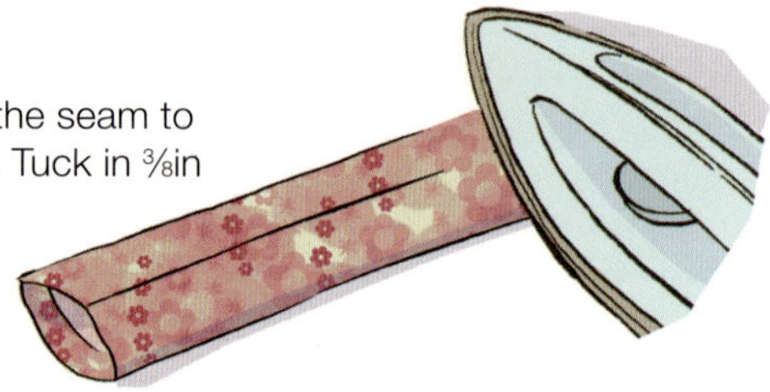

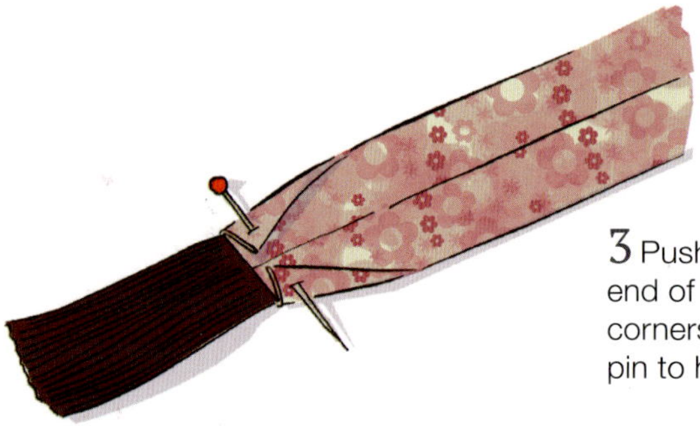

3 Push ⅜in (1cm) of elastic into one end of the tube. On the back, fold the corners of the fabric in, as shown, and pin to hold the folds.

4 Sewing either by hand or machine, sew back and forth across the fabric a couple of times. Sew the other end of elastic into the other end of the tube to make a hairband. Check that the hairband isn't twisted before you sew. The folded layers of fabric plus the elastic are quite thick, so use a thimble to help you push the needle through if you're hand-sewing, and sew slowly if you're using a machine.

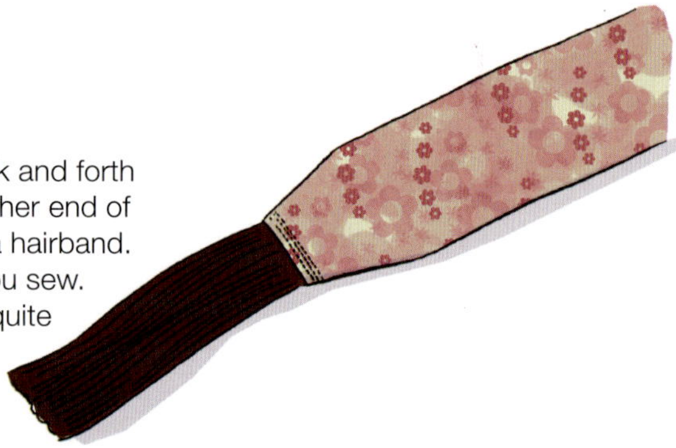

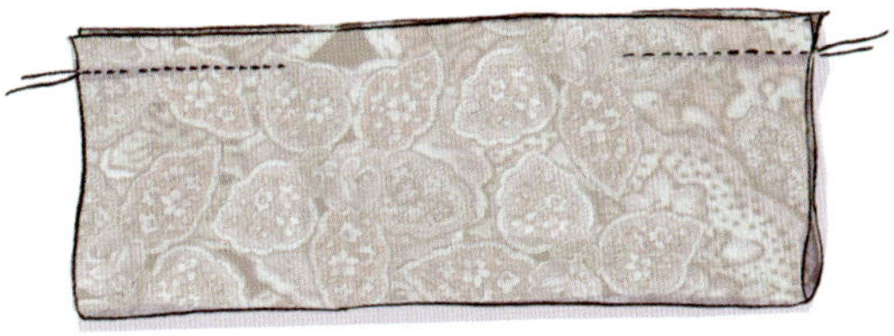

5 Right side in, fold one of the large bow pieces in half lengthwise. From each end and taking a ⅜-in (1-cm) seam allowance, sew a short length of the seam, so that there is a 2-in (5-cm) gap in the middle.

6 Roll the seam to center back and press the tube flat, pressing the seam allowances open. Taking the same seam allowance, sew across the short ends, then cut off the corners within the seam allowances (see page 86). Turn right side out, pushing out the corners neatly, and press. Make up the second large bow piece the same way, but fold it in half widthwise.

7 Stack the shorter, wider piece on top of the longer thinner one, centering them. Using doubled sewing thread, stitch a line of short gathering stitches across the middle of the bow-to-be, sewing through all layers.

8 Pull the gathers up as tightly as possible to make a bow. Secure the thread by stitching back and forth a few times through the gathered section.

9 Follow Steps 1–2 to make the small bow piece into a tiny tube. Wrap the tube around the middle of the bow and sew the ends together at center back. (If it's a bit loose, just tuck a bit more of one end in before sewing up.)

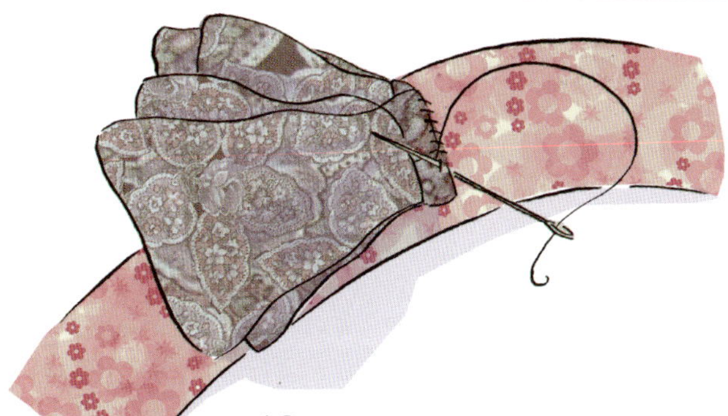

10 Sewing through the back of the bow center, sew the bow to the hairband. I've sewn mine on at a jaunty angle, but you could go Minnie Mouse-style and perch your bow right on top.

Patchwork dog coat

Your dog is bound to vary in size and shape to my Elvis, but this is a simple coat pattern that can be adjusted to suit any size of pooch. And while I've gone for a simplified version of crazy patchwork that's doable for novice sewcalists, you can use as many fabrics as you want, and add as many embellishments as you want to make your dog a coat of many colors.

YOU'RE GOING TO NEED...

- Diagram on page 92
- Piece of backing fabric the size of the coat: see Customizing the Pattern, below
- Tape measure, pencil, and ruler
- Scraps of fabric for patchwork
- Fabric scissors
- Hand-sewing needle
- Basting thread: I always use ordinary sewing thread in a contrast color
- Pins
- Sewing threads to match fabrics
- Sewing machine
- Iron and ironing board
- Scraps of trimming and iron-on patches
- Enough ¾-in (2-cm) wide bias binding to go right around the circumference of the coat
- Two snap fastenings

CUSTOMIZING THE PATTERN

On the diagram on page 92 there are arrows telling you which bits of your dog to measure so that you can draw out your own pattern to fit. I advise cutting a coat from newspaper first and making sure it will fit before starting work on the fabric.

1 Using a pencil and ruler, draw out the pattern on the backing fabric. You can draw around the base of a mug or small plate (depending on the scale of your coat) to create the curves. Cut it out roughly, leaving about ¾in (2cm) all around.

Making the patchwork

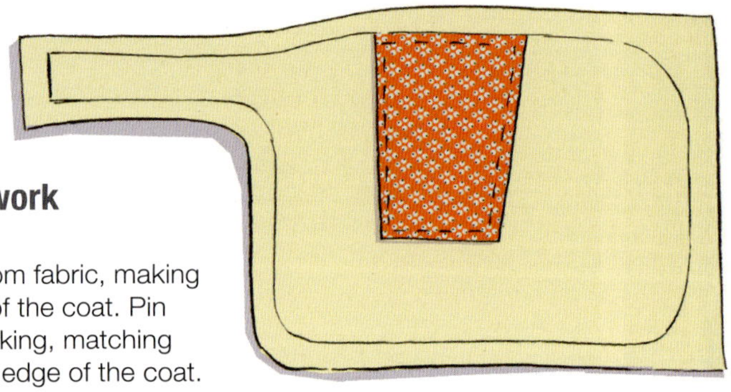

2 Cut the first patch from fabric, making it about half the width of the coat. Pin then baste it to the backing, matching one edge to the drawn edge of the coat. (I always baste the first patch as I find it makes life easier, but I don't baste any others.)

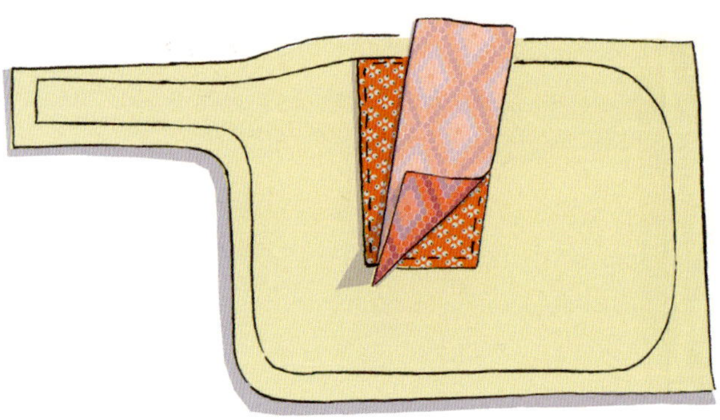

3 Cut a second patch that's a bit longer than the first one. Lay it right side down on the first patch, matching one side edge and with some fabric overlapping at each end.

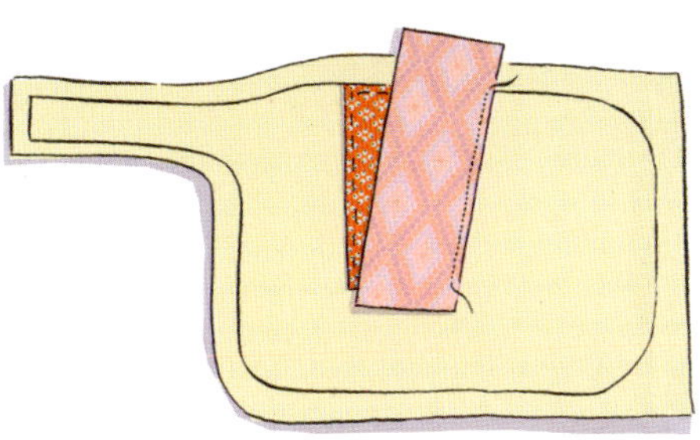

4 Sew the patches to the backing fabric, taking a ⅜-in (1-cm) seam allowance.

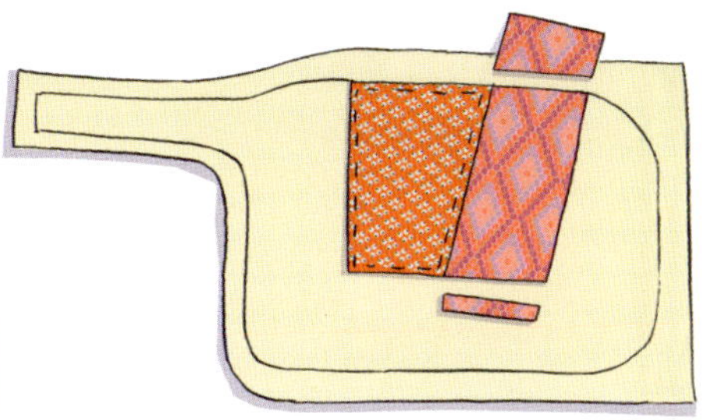

5 Fold the second patch out flat and press. Use the pencil and ruler to mark off the edges of the second patch to align with the first, then cut off the excess fabric.

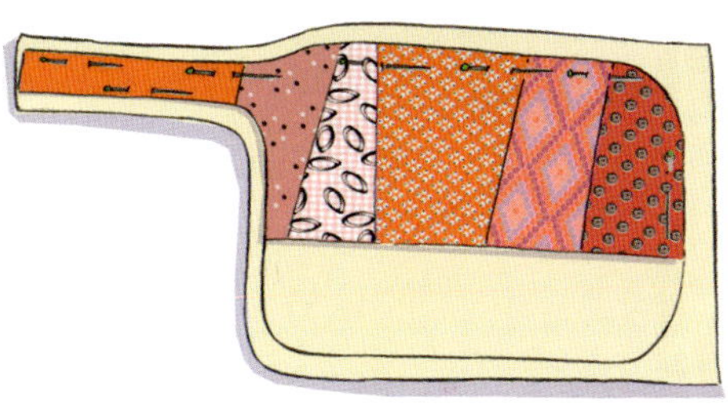

6 Continue in this way to cover one half of the coat with patched fabric, including the chest strap. Pin the patches in place around the outer edges. Remove the basting stitches.

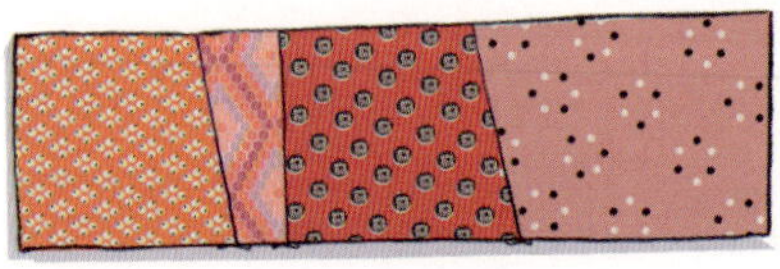

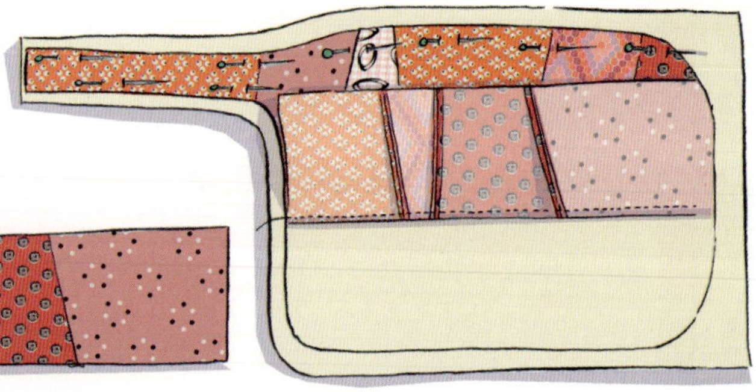

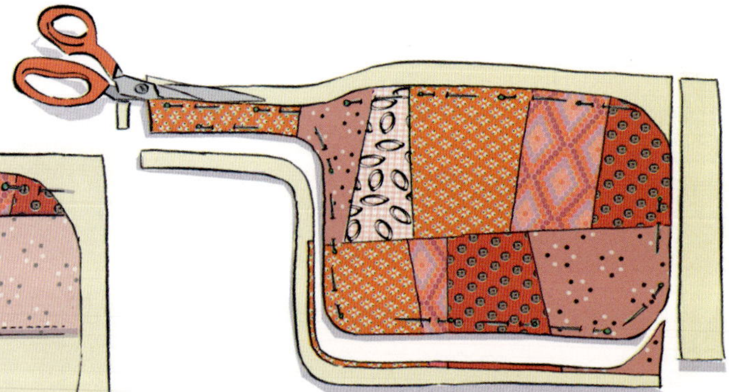

7 Taking ⅜-in (1-cm) seam allowances, piece together some fabrics to make a strip wide enough to cover the other half of the coat. Press all the seam allowances open.

8 Pin then sew the strip to the top section of the coat in the same way as for the previous patches. You can offset the seam a bit so that it won't run in a straight line down the dog's spine. Press the strip flat onto the backing and pin it around the outer edges.

9 Cut out the coat from the backing fabric, following your drawn edge. Set the sewing machine to a medium zigzag stitch and sew all around the edges, sewing all the patches to the backing.

Making the coat

10 At this stage, try the coat on your dog, safety pinning the chest strap closed. If your hound has a roundish derrière—as Elvis does—then you might want to put a dart in to improve fit. I've made a dart that's 1¼in (3cm) wide at the base and 4¾in (12cm) long. Press the dart to one side.

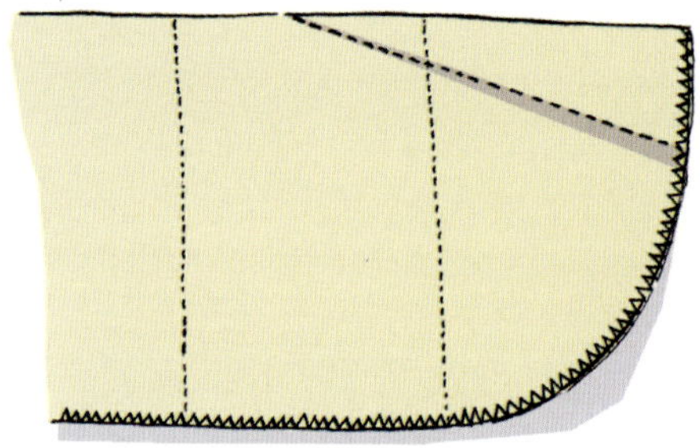

11 You can add some trimmings: I've chosen a little pom-pom trim around the neckline. Just baste it on at this stage.

12 Iron the bias binding in half along its length. Fold in and iron ⅜in (1cm) at one end. Starting halfway along the top of the chest strap, slip the folded binding over the edge of the fabric. Topstitch the binding in place, sewing ⅛in (3mm) in from the folded binding edge, to the end of the strap.

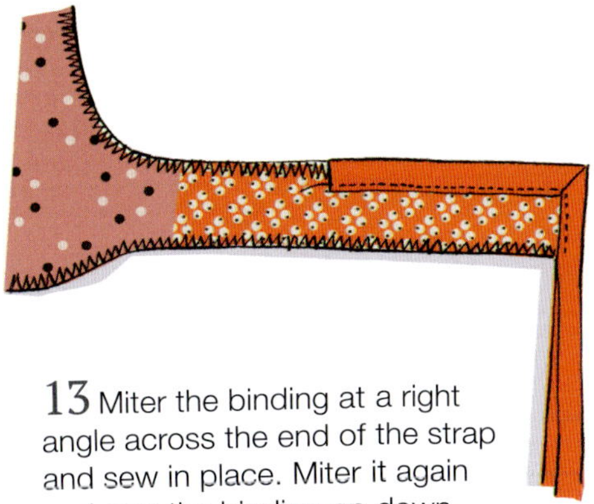

13 Miter the binding at a right angle across the end of the strap and sew in place. Miter it again and sew the binding on down the other side of the strap and continue around the rest of the coat.

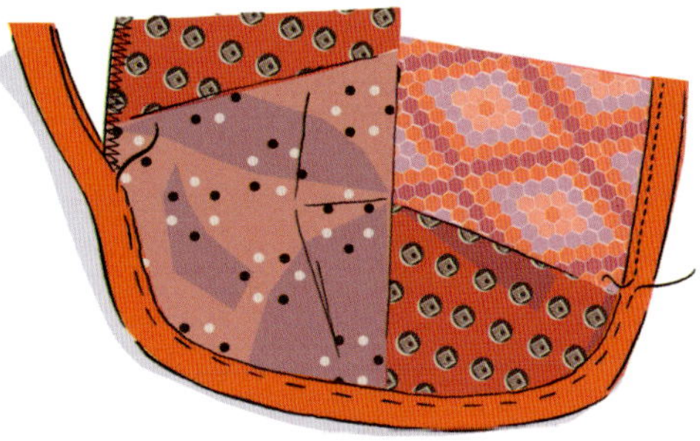

14 At the curved end of the coat, I found it best to stop machine sewing and baste the binding around the curves, using lots of steam from the iron and stretching the folded edge with my fingers to make a neat curve. Once it's basted in place, topstitch as before.

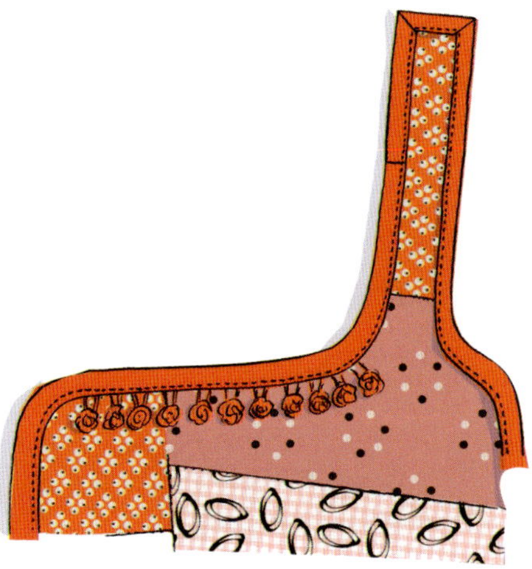

15 At the back neck the binding covers the band of the pom-pom trim neatly. When you get close to the starting point, trim the binding ⅜in (1cm) longer than needed, fold in the end, butt it up to the starting point, and topstitch over it.

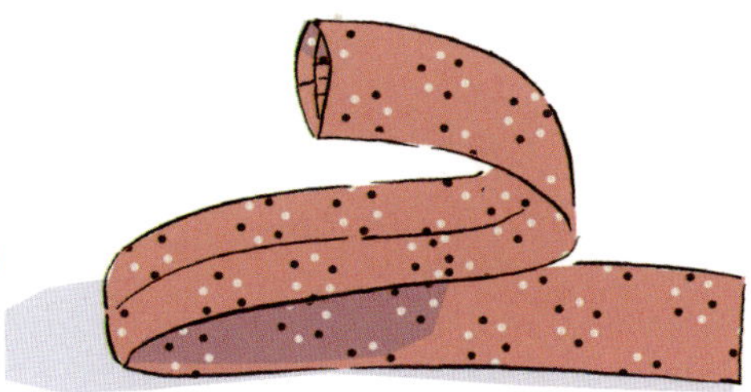

16 Cut a strip of fabric long enough to be a tummy strap and twice as wide as needed plus ¾in (2cm). Follow Steps 1–2 of Big Bow (see page 62) to make a tube with tucked-in ends.

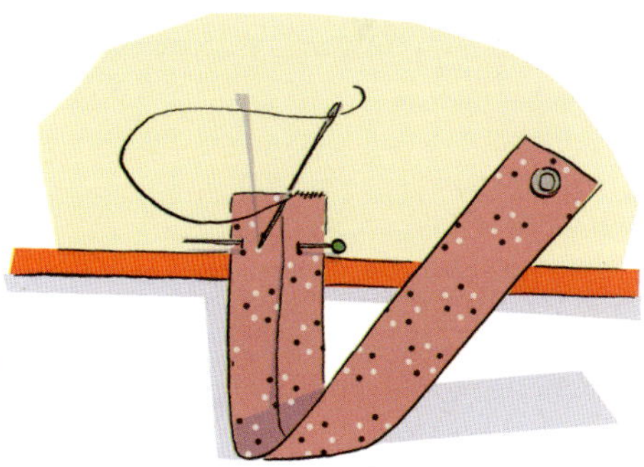

17 Try the coat on your dog again and pin the tummy strap in position on the inside of the coat, being careful not to stab the pooch with the pin. Sew the strap on with firm whip stitches (see page 87), sewing through the lining only. Fix a snap fastening to the other end of the strap.

18 Fit the other end of the snap fastening to the other side of the coat to align with the strap. I covered the back of the snap with an iron-on embroidered patch. Fit snaps to the end of the chest strap and front edge of the coat in the same way.

Big obi belt

A version of a Japanese obi belt, this is a very quick project to make, and ideal for using up smallish pieces of fabric left over from dressmaking projects. Made a dress with contrast cuffs and collar? Make a big belt to coordinate with it. The tassel I've added is a nod to the traditional netsuke worn with obi belts; you can add any charm or decoration you like, or none at all.

YOU'RE GOING TO NEED...

- Two pieces of fabric cut to your waist measurement (but you may wish to make them 2in (5cm) longer for comfort—you can then overlap the ends if needed when the belt is worn), by a width you feel comfortable wearing, plus ⅜-in (1-cm) seam allowances all around: my fabric is 5½in (14cm) wide for a finished belt 4¾in (12cm) wide
- One piece of heavyweight fusible interfacing the same size as the fabric
- Fabric scissors
- Iron and ironing board
- Fading fabric marker
- Pins
- Sewing threads to match fabric and ribbon
- Sewing machine
- Hand-sewing needle
- Point turner or butter knife
- Tassel or charm (optional)
- 3yd (3m) of ⅝-in (1.5-cm) wide ribbon
- Basting thread: I always use ordinary sewing thread in a contrast color

1 Iron the fusible interfacing onto the back of the fabric that will be the right side of the belt. Using the fabric marker, round off the corners, as shown (I drew around the edge of my coffee cup).

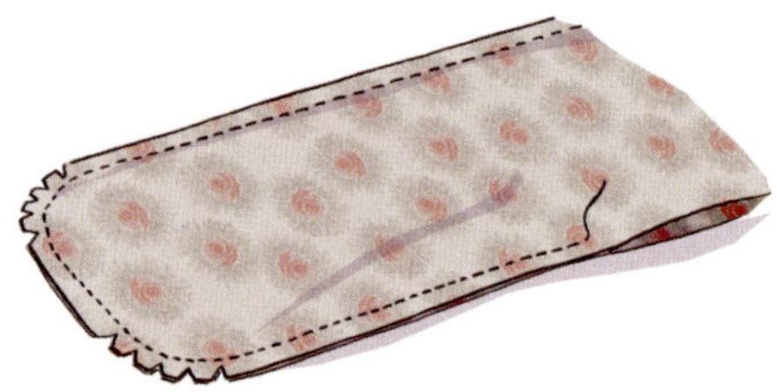

2 Place the pieces of fabric right sides together and pin. Taking a ⅜-in (1-cm) seam allowance, machine-sew right around the belt, following the drawn lines at the corners and leaving a 4-in (10-cm) gap in one long edge. Take out the pins. Clip notches in the seam allowances around the curves, spacing them about ¼in (6mm) apart and cutting to within ⅛in (3mm) of the stitching (see page 86). Trim all the seam allowances to ¼in (6mm), other than across the open gap.

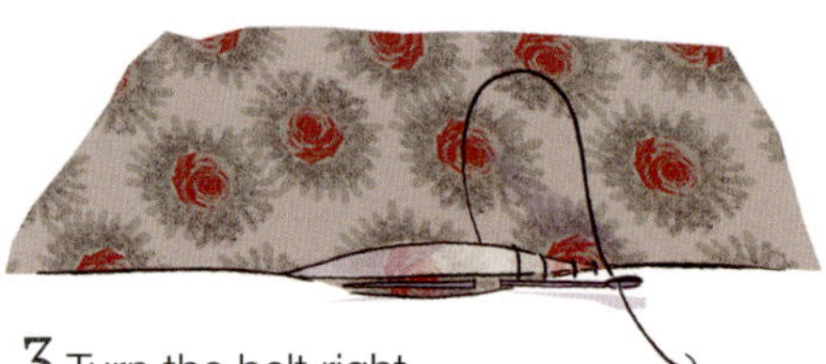

3 Turn the belt right side out through the gap, carefully pushing out the corners to be smoothly rounded (a butter knife is useful here if you don't have a bespoke point turner). Ladder stitch (see page 88) the gap closed.

4 If you want to add a "netsuke," then thread it onto a ribbon or cord that's twice the desired hanging length, plus ⅜in (1cm). I've used a piece of the tying ribbon and basted the raw ends together.

STITCHING ON THE EDGE

It does take a bit of practice to edge-stitch beautifully, and the best way to master the technique is on lined paper. Slip the paper under the foot, then turn the sewing machine hand wheel to lower the needle until it is touching a line on the paper. Note the position of the toes of the foot in relation to the line. Sew along the line, watching the position of the toes rather than the up-and-down movement of the needle, as that will be distracting. Most sewing machines allow you to move the needle position left to right, so you can align the line on the paper with the edge of a toe of the foot, then move the needle until it is on the line. Sew as many straight lines as you need to to feel comfortable with the technique, then change the needle (sewing paper will blunt it), and sew on the ribbon.

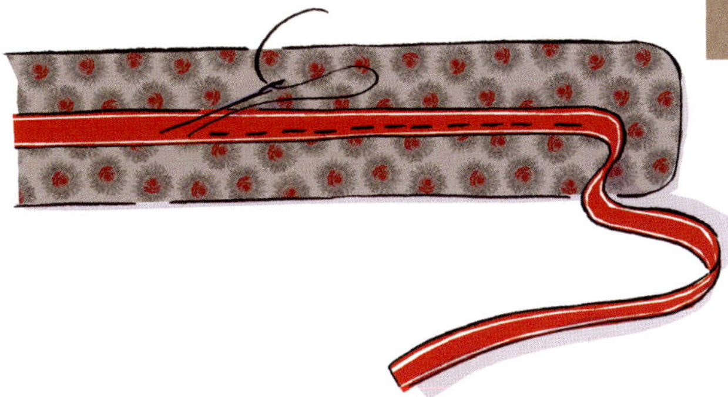

5 Pin the ribbon to the right side of the belt, centering it top to bottom and with an equal amount free at each end for tying. Tuck ⅜in (1cm) of the hanging loop of the netsuke under the edge of the ribbon: I placed mine a little to one side of the middle of the belt so that it will hang to one side when the belt is worn. Starting 4in (10cm) from one end of the belt, baste the ribbon in place, sewing right along to the other end of the belt. Remove the pins.

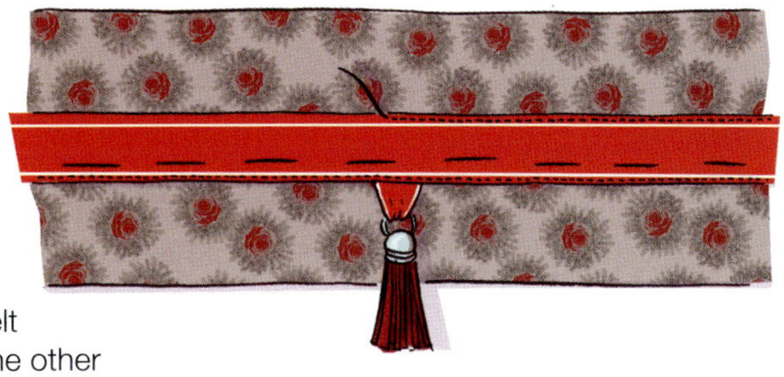

6 Using thread to match the ribbon, and sewing very slowly and carefully, machine-sew along the lower edge of the ribbon, stitching right on the edge. Follow the basting, so that the stitching starts 4in (10cm) from one end of the belt and continues right along to the other end. Repeat along the top edge.

7 To wear the belt, wrap it around your waist with the ends at the back, tucking the free end under the ribboned end if the ends do not meet exactly, then wrap the ribbons around to the front and tie them in a bow. You can trim the ends of the ribbon if need be.

Sew-on patches

In my school's 1970s production of Joseph and the Amazing Technicolor Dreamcoat, the eponymous garment was a denim jean jacket covered in embroidered patches, lovingly stitched on by Mrs Chewins, proud mother of Joseph, aka Max. As a lowly member of the Egyptian chorus (and one asked to mime rather than actually sing, as my tone-deaf vocals put off those around me), I was deeply, deeply jealous of that jacket. So I'm thrilled that the "goes around, comes around" nature of fashion has brought us these patches once again (and jean jackets have never really gone away). My patches let you use up the tiniest scraps of gorgeous printed fabrics, and they look brilliant mixed in with purchased embroidered patches, too.

YOU'RE GOING TO NEED...

- Scraps of fabric, fusible interfacing, and fusible webbing: the fabric must be able to withstand a hot iron, so I recommend printed cotton
- Iron and ironing board
- Fading fabric marker
- Fabric scissors
- Sewing threads to match fabrics
- Sewing machine
- Pencil

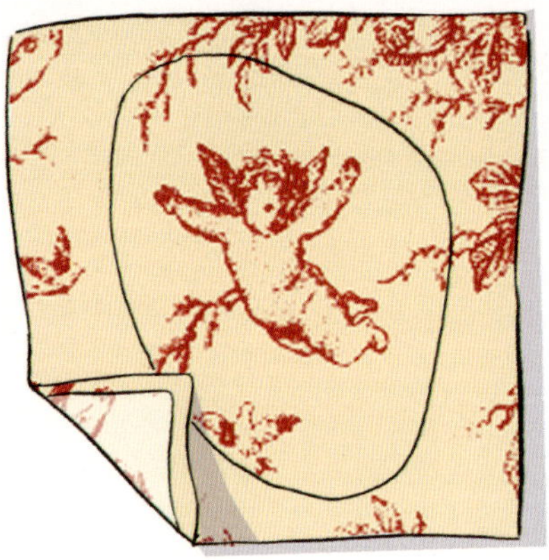

1 Iron a piece of fusible interfacing onto the back of the piece of fabric you want to use. On the right side, draw out the shape of the patch. Don't make very tight curves as they'll be difficult to satin stitch neatly around.

2 Set the sewing machine to satin stitch: a very tight, medium-width zigzag stitch (see page 88 for how to stitch this by hand). You might want to experiment with this on spare bits of fabric if it's new to you. Satin stitch around the drawn line. If you need to pivot the fabric, stop sewing with the needle down on the outer edge of the stitching; that will help keep the outline of the patch smooth.

3 Very carefully cut out the shape around the edge of the stitching, being sure not to cut through any stitches. For a super-neat finish, work another ring of satin stitch over the first one, so that the stitches overlap the cut edge and cover any trace of fabric there. But this really is optional.

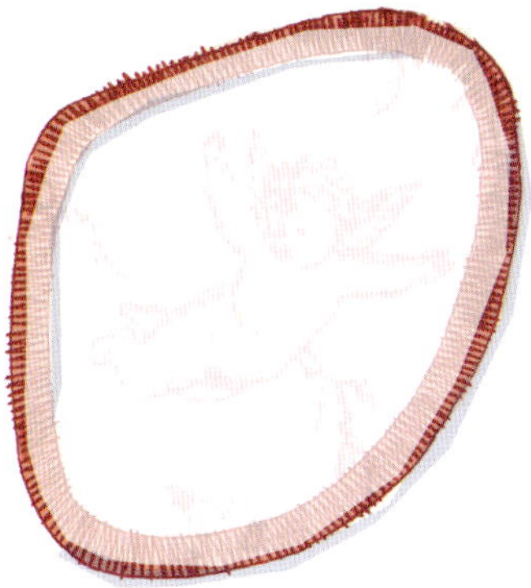

4 Lay the patch face down on a scrap of fusible webbing and draw around it with a pencil. Cut out the shape just inside the drawn line. Place the webbing right side down on the back of the patch, check that it overlaps the stitching (tuck the ends of thread under it to secure them), and trim any bits that protrude, then iron the webbing in place.

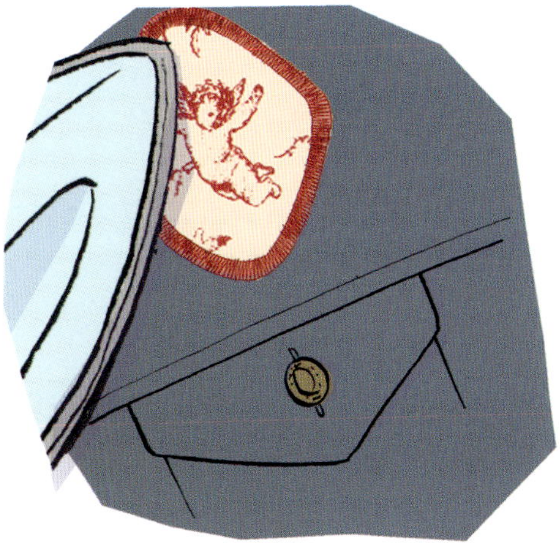

5 To attach the patch to a jacket (or anything else), peel off the paper backing and iron it in place. You can add a few stitches, sewing over the satin stitches, if need be.

CHAPTER 4

For Crafters

Sewing kit

This really is the most amazingly useful piece of kit, especially if, like me, you love hand-sewing in front of a good movie on the television. Hang this pincushion over the arm of your chair, and you have pins and scissors to hand, plus a repository for all the scraps of thread that otherwise find their way onto the floor. Or you can stash small tools and notions in the bag. It's quite a long project, as there are various elements to make, but nothing is complicated.

YOU'RE GOING TO NEED...

- Two pieces of fabric and one piece of heavyweight interfacing, each measuring 10½x 6⅛in (26.5 x 15.5cm) for the thread bag: I used needlecord fabric throughout
- Two pieces of fabric measuring 8 x 10in (20 x 25cm) for the base
- One piece of fabric measuring 2¾ x 4¼in (7 x 10.5cm) for the pocket
- One piece of fabric measuring 1¾x 12in (4.5 x 30cm) for the loop
- Two pieces of fabric measuring 10 x 4in (25 x 10cm) for the pincushion
- Button
- Polyester toy filling
- Tape measure
- Fabric scissors
- Iron and ironing board
- Pins
- Sewing threads to match fabrics
- Sewing machine
- Fabric marker
- Small plate
- Hand-sewing needle
- Two door hinges, or something else flat and heavy to use as a weight for the pincushion

1 Iron the interfacing onto the back of the inner thread bag. Fold the piece in half widthwise and, taking a ⅜-in (1-cm) seam allowance, sew the seam. Don't interface the outer bag, but sew it in the same way. Trim the seam allowances to half their width on the inner. Roll the seam allowances to just off center back—so that when the two pieces are put together the seams are staggered—and press them open.

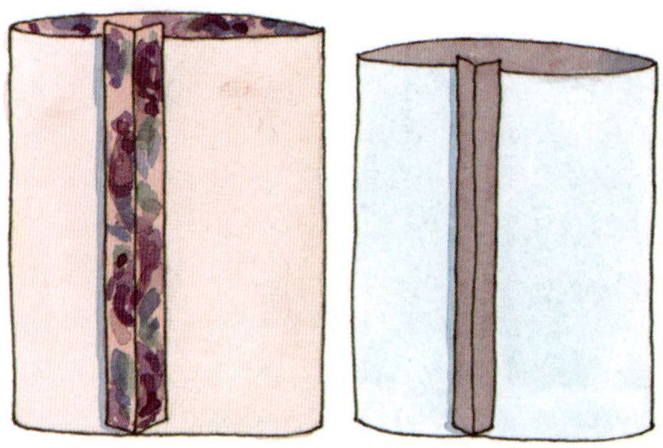

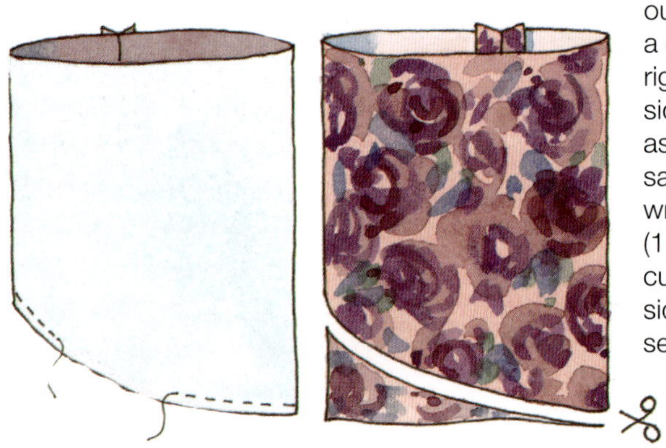

2 Turn the outer bag right side out and cut the bottom edge into a curve, curving down from left to right. Leave the inner bag wrong side out, and use the outer bag as a template to cut it to the same shape. Turn the outer bag wrong side out and, taking a ⅜-in (1-cm) seam allowance, sew the curved base. Then turn it right side out again. Sew the curved seam of the inner bag, but leave a 2-in (5-cm) gap in the middle of the seam.

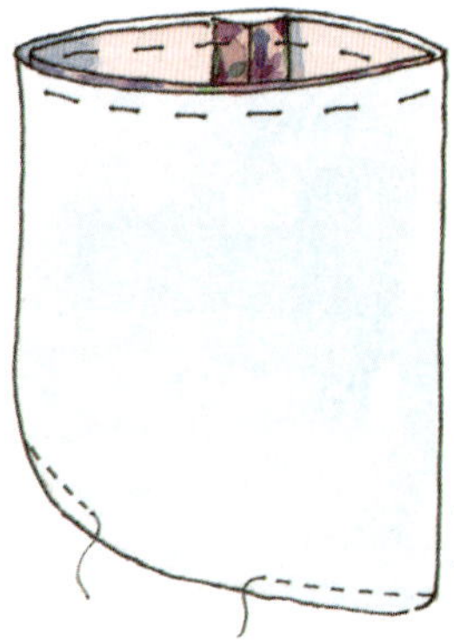

3 Slip the outer bag into the inner, so the right sides are together. Baste and then sew the layers together around the top edge, taking a ⅜-in (1-cm) seam allowance.

4 Turn the bag right side out through the gap in the lining, pulling the outer bag through, then continuing to pull until the whole piece is right side out. Press it flat, pressing under the seam allowances across the gap. Ladder stitch (see page 88) the gap closed.

5 Turn the inner bag down inside the outer, pushing out the corner and curve smoothly. Topstitch around the top edge of the bag, sewing ⅛in (2–3mm) in from the edge. Sew the button to the center back of the inner bag, ⅝in (1.5cm) down from the top edge.

6 Zigzag or serge (overlock) one short edge of the pocket piece. Press under a ⅜-in (1-cm) hem on that edge. Sewing ⅜in (1cm) in from each raw side edge, sew across the hem, as shown. Clip off the corners of the hem (see page 86).

7 Turn the hem right side out and press it flat. Press under and baste (tack) a ⅜-in (1-cm) hem all around the pocket, mitering the two bottom corners.

8 Right side in, fold the loop strip in half lengthwise. Taking a ⅜-in (1-cm) seam allowance, sew the long edge. Turn the tube right side out (see page 86). With the seam along one edge, press the tube flat.

9 Round off the left-hand bottom corner of the base pieces: I drew around a small plate. Position the pocket on the right side of a base piece, 1¼in (3cm) in from both the side and the bottom edges of the square right-hand bottom corner. Topstitch it in place, then take out the basting stitches. Fold the loop in half, overlapping the ends so that the wrong side of one end lies on top of the right side of the other end, and baste the raw edges to the top edge of the base, 1½in (4cm) from the left-hand edge. Pin the length of the loop to the base to keep it out of the way of the stitching.

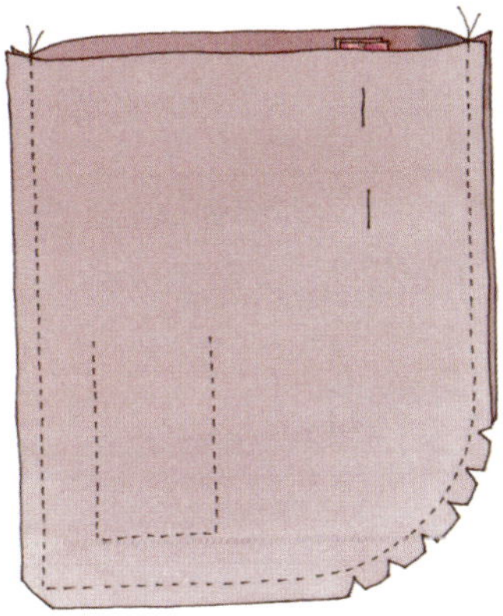

10 Lay the other base piece right side down on top of the first one, matching all raw edges. Taking a ⅜-in (1-cm) seam allowance, sew all around the edges, but leave the top straight edge open. Clip the curves (see page 86) and turn the base right side out. Press the seams flat.

11 Lay one pincushion piece flat, right side up. Lay the base right side down centered the far edge of the pincushion piece, as shown. Baste the edges together. Lay the other pincushion piece right side down on top of the first, matching all edges. Pin the layers together along the top edge.

12 Roll the base up as tightly as possible and tuck it in between the pincushion pieces. Pin the pincushion pieces together all around, enclosing the rolled-up base.

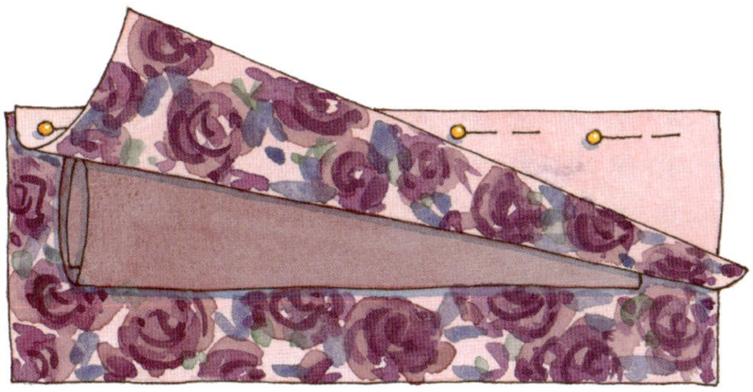

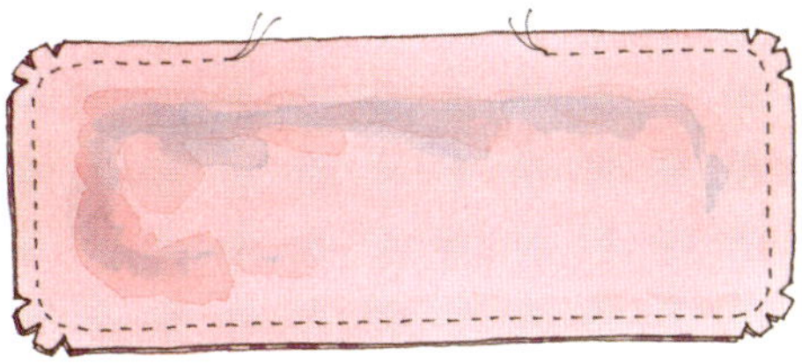

13 Taking a ⅜-in (1-cm) seam allowance, sew the pincushion seams, making the corners gently rounded and leaving a 3-in (8-cm) gap in the middle of the edge the base is basted to. Clip the curves.

14 Turn the pincushion right side out through the gap, unrolling the base piece. Press everything, apart from the loop, flat, pressing under the seam allowances across the gap. Fold the pincushion forward over the top edge of the base, into the position it will sit in when finished. Slip the door hinges in through the gap, positioning them to lie flat along the underside of the pincushion.

15 Fill the pincushion with plenty of stuffing, pushing it in on top of the hinges until the pincushion is firm. Ladder stitch (see page 88) the gap closed. Button the bag onto the loop.

Knitter's bucket bag

This is the perfect project bag: seriously. It's deep enough to hold lots of balls of yarn, but not huge and unwieldy. It's got a flat bottom so it will stand up, and a handle you can make whichever length you like for a bag. It has pockets for knitting needles and other kit, and a loop for dropped-stitch-emergency safety pins and stitch holders. And it's good-looking, and quick and easy to make in your favorite colors: or if you are super-geek coordinated, in colors to match your knitting project…

YOU'RE GOING TO NEED…

- Piece of thick fabric measuring 5 x 10¼in (13 x 26cm), for knitting needle pocket: you can make this wider to hold more sets of needles if you want
- One piece of furnishing-weight fabric measuring 23 x 16in (58 x 40cm), for the body of the bag, and one measuring 16½ x 4½in (42 x 11cm), for the handle: this was the length I liked, you can adjust it to suit you
- Circle of thick fabric, 8in (20cm) in diameter: I used a chenille furnishing fabric
- Circle of cotton fabric, 8in (20cm) in diameter and piece measuring 23 x 16in (58 x 40cm), for the lining
- Small pieces of fabric for inside pocket/s: make as many as you want at whatever sizes you want
- Piece of ribbon for safety-pin loop
- Fabric scissors
- Iron and ironing board
- Pins
- Sewing threads to match fabrics
- Sewing machine
- Masking tape
- Hand-sewing needle

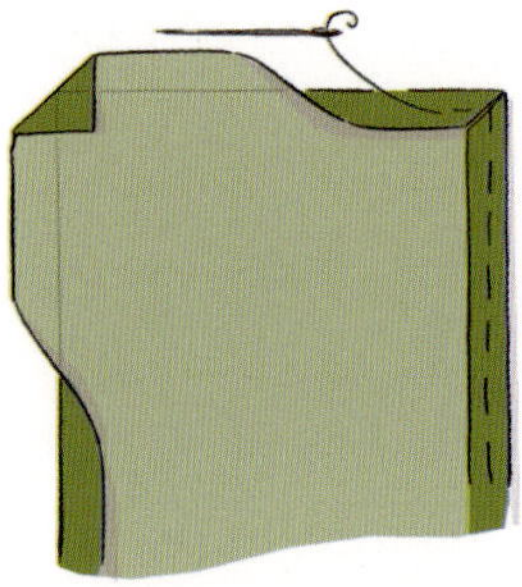

1 Start by making the needle pocket. If your fabric will fray, zigzag or serge the edges (mine didn't fray). Press under a ⅜in (1cm) hem all around. At the corners, fold over the point at the pressed lines, then fold in the hems to make a neat miter; baste the hems and miters in place.

2 Sew the top hem of the pocket piece and fasten off the threads on the back. Lay the bag body fabric flat and right side up, with the long edges at the top and bottom. Pin the pocket in position: you can place it wherever you like, mine is pretty much centered. Topstitching ¼in (6mm) in from the edges, sew around three sides of the pocket, reversing at the top corners for strength. Fasten off the threads on the back.

3 Use masking tape to mark out the lines of stitching that will divide the pocket: I've measured ¾in (2cm) in from each side, so the middle section will be wider, to hold thicker needles. Sew along the outside edge of each piece of tape, reversing at the top for strength. Fasten off the threads on the back.

4 Fold the bag piece in half and, taking a ⅜-in (1-cm) seam allowance, sew the two short ends together to form a tube. Zigzag the seam allowance.

5 Right sides together and taking a ⅜-in (1-cm) seam allowance, pin and then baste the circle of thick fabric into the bottom of the bag. Sew the seam, then zigzag stitch and trim, or serge, the seam allowance.

6 Make up the lining in the same way as the main bag. You can add as many pockets as you like to the inside of the bag. I like to have a loop of ribbon on to which I pin stitch holders, and a safety pin that I can find quickly if I drop a stitch. Leave a 4-in (10-cm) gap in the base seam for turning the bag through.

7 Right side in, fold the handle strip in half lengthwise and sew the seam, taking a ⅜-in (1-cm) seam allowance. Zigzag stitch and trim, or serge, the seam allowance. Turn the handle right side out (see page 86), roll the seam to center back, then press the handle flat.

8 Right sides together, pin the ends of the handle to the sides of the main bag, positioning them opposite one another and as you want in relation to the pocket position. Check that the handle isn't twisted. Set the sewing machine to a small zigzag stitch and sew across each end of the handle to attach it to the bag.

9 Right sides together (so the main bag is right side out and the lining is right side in), slip the main bag into the lining. Match the raw top edges of both pieces, making sure the handle is tucked down out of the way.

10 Sew around the top edges, taking a ⅜-in (1-cm) seam allowance. Zigzag stitch and trim, or serge, the seam allowance.

11 Gently pull the main bag right side out through the gap in the lining, then continue pulling until the lining is right-side out, too. Ladder stitch (see page 88) the gap in the lining closed. Tuck the lining back into the bag and you're done.

Patchwork pincushion

Another piece of sewing kit that's both cute and practical, this is a traditional pincushion design that looks perky in vintage or new fabrics. It's entirely hand-sewn, so makes an excellent lap project in front of a great movie on the television. (I won't try and recommend one in particular, but avoid anything too exciting, as distraction can lead to finger-stabbing with needles and pins.) And if you stuff the patchwork firmly and stop at Step 3, the resulting ball is a great baby toy.

YOU'RE GOING TO NEED...

- Pentagon templates on page 92
- 12 scraps of fabric measuring at least 2¾in (7cm) square
- Paper for templates
- Paper and fabric scissors
- Pins
- Basting thread: I always use ordinary sewing thread in a contrast color
- Hand-sewing needle
- Sewing threads to match fabrics
- Toy stuffing
- Two buttons
- Very long sewing needle, such as a doll needle
- Strong sewing thread, such as buttonhole thread

1 Using the pentagon templates (not the hexagon ones) and following Steps 1–8 of Hexie Cushion (see pages 14–15), sew five pentagons to the edges of one central one. Because of the five-sided shape, the result will be a cup, rather than a flat patchwork. Make two the same.

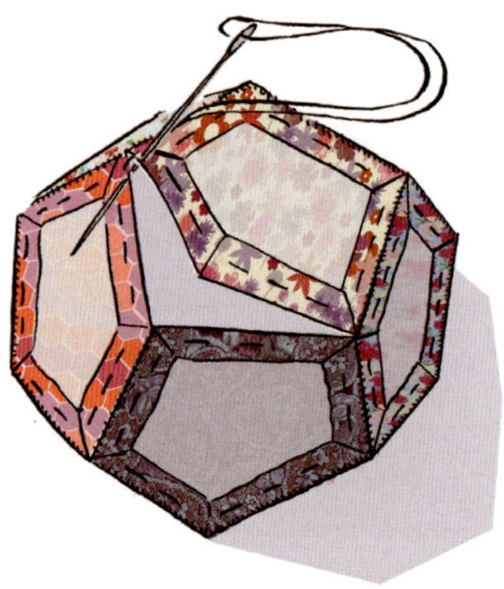

2 Fit the two cups together to make a ball, and sew them around the central seam, in the same way you sewed the pentagons together, leaving two edges open, as shown, but don't fasten off or cut the thread. Take out all the basting stitches and papers.

3 Turn the ball right side out, then fill it with toy stuffing. You need to stuff the ball fairly firmly for a pincushion—and firmer still if it's going to be a toy ball. Ladder stitch (see page 88) the gap closed and secure the thread.

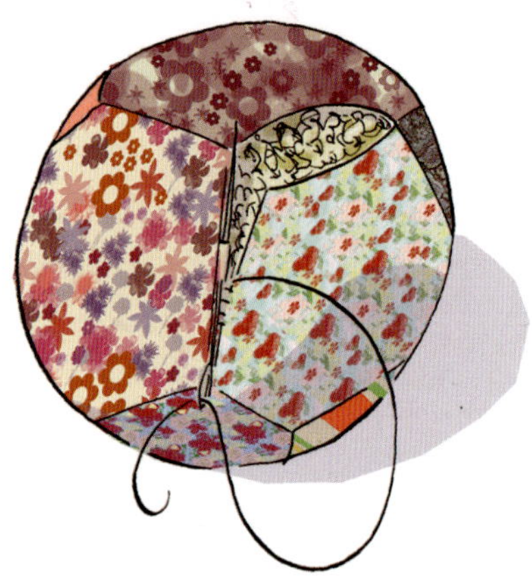

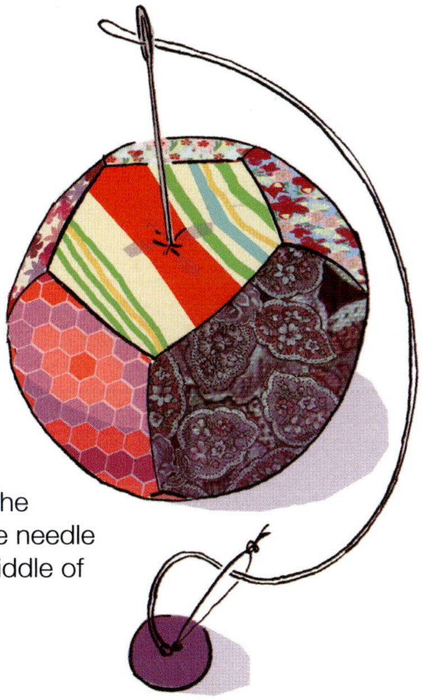

4 Thread the long needle with a long length of strong thread, double it, and knot the ends. From the back, take the needle through a hole in a button, then back through the other hole and between the threads above the knot. Pull tight, then push the needle straight down through the middle of the pincushion.

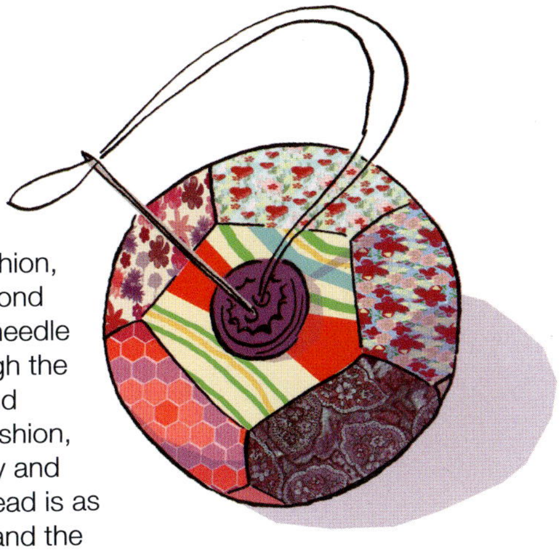

5 On the other side of the pincushion, thread on the second button. Take the needle back down through the other hole in it, and through the pincushion, then pull smoothly and firmly until the thread is as tight as possible and the buttons are deeply indented into the pincushion.

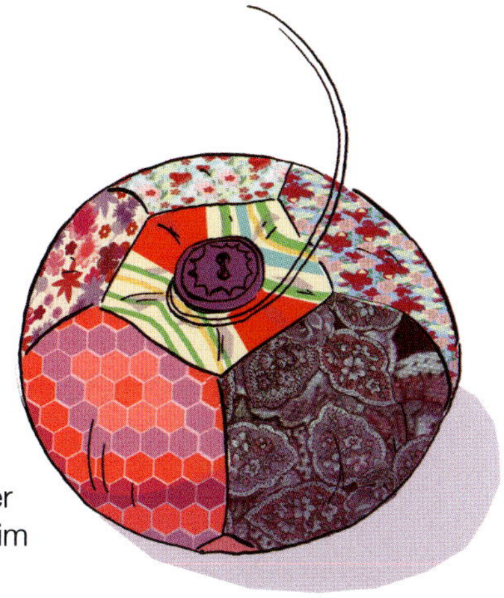

6 Wrap the thread around under the first button a couple of times to keep the tension, then stitch back and forth through the buttons and pincushion a few times. Secure the thread by wrapping and tying it under one of the buttons, then trim the ends.

Knitting needle storage roll

If you absolutely cannot resist nice-looking knitting needles and have ended up with a needle stash that rivals your yarn stash, then a bespoke roll is exactly what you need to keep them organized. You can store needles by sizes, materials (my preferred system), colors... whatever works for you.

YOU'RE GOING TO NEED...

- One piece of medium-weight main fabric measuring 16 x 18½in (40 x 47cm), for the back and one piece measuring 16 x 10¾in (40 x 27cm), for the front: I used needlecord
- One piece of lightweight contrast fabric measuring 16 x 10in (40 x 25cm): I used cotton
- Iron and ironing board
- Pins
- Sewing threads to match fabrics
- Sewing machine
- Fabric scissors
- Rotary cutter with pinking blade and cutting mat, or pinking shears
- Masking tape, or fading fabric marker, or quilting guide
- Strong sewing thread to match main fabric: I used topstitching thread
- Hand-sewing needle
- Button with a shank
- Cord long enough to wrap around the rolled-up roll a few times: I used 23½in (60cm) of leather

HOW MUCH FABRIC?

I've given the fabric sizes for this roll, which measures 15in (38cm) long when rolled out flat and holds needles up to 12in (30cm) long, but you can adjust sizes to suit your needle collection.

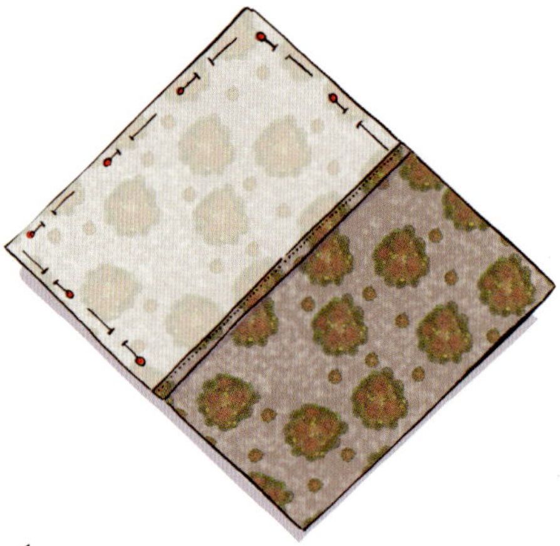

1 Turn under and sew a double ⅜in (1cm) hem on one long edge of the front piece of main fabric. Lay it right sides together onto the back piece, matching raw edges around three sides. Pin it in place.

2 Lay the contrast piece right sides together on the exposed half of the back piece, so that one edge overlaps the hemmed edge of the front, as shown. (To reduce bulk I used the selvage for this edge, or you can overcast or serge the edge to finish it.) Pin the layers together all around the edges.

3 Taking a ⅜-in (1-cm) seam allowance, sew all around the edges. I sewed a wavy edge across what will be the flap, sewing the shape freehand; you can draw a shape onto the fabric first, or leave the flap edge straight if you prefer. Pink the seam allowance to finish it and reduce bulk. Clip the corners (see page 86).

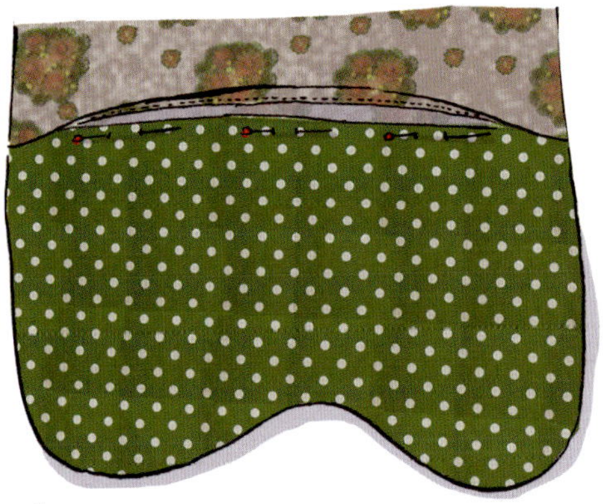

4 Turn the roll right sides out through the overlapped edges and smooth the selvage/neatened edge of the contrast fabric flat under the hemmed edge. (This might sound a bit mysterious if you are just reading through, but when you come to do this it will make sense.) Keeping the hemmed edge rolled back out of the way, pin the selvage/neatened edge in place and machine-sew a straight line across the edge to hold it flat. You won't be able to get right to the ends, but that doesn't matter; just sew as far as you can.

5 Decide on the sizes for the needle pockets. You can lay your needles in position and pin around them if you want: I made most of my pockets 1⅜in (3.5cm) wide, and two pockets 2in (5cm) wide. You can mark the pocket positions with strips of masking tape, or lines drawn with a fading fabric marker, or you can use a quilting guide as you sew.

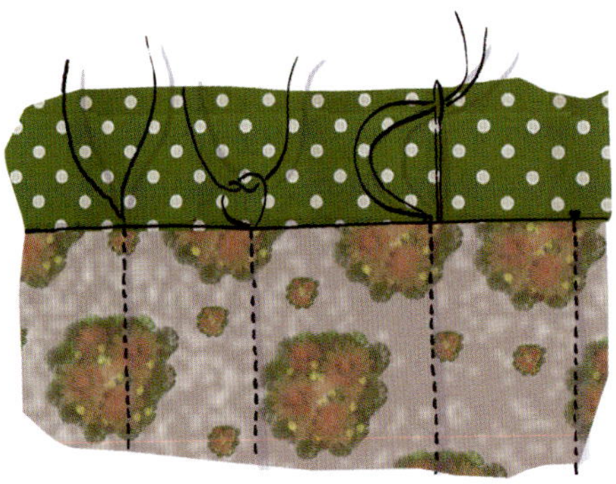

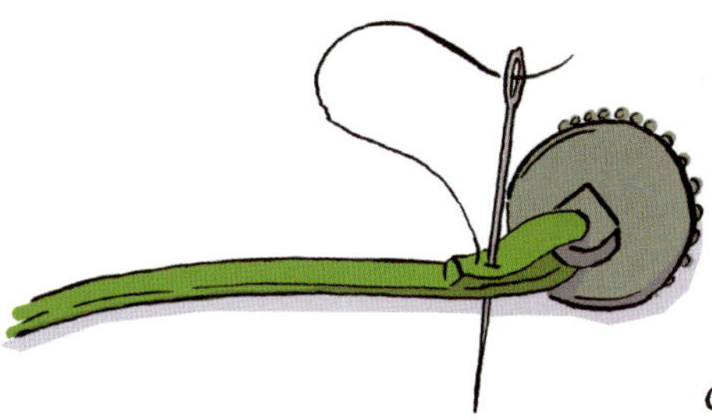

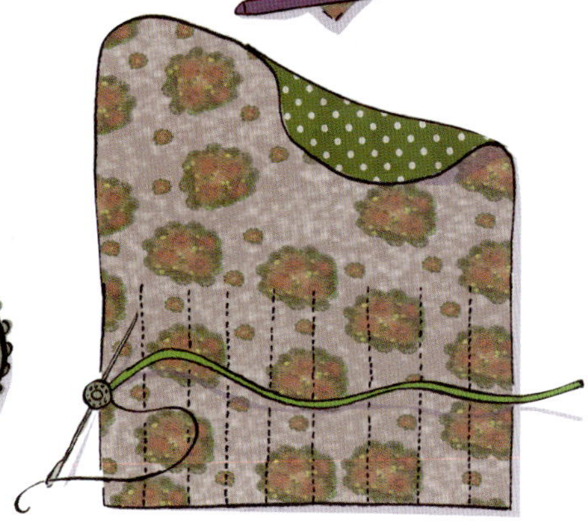

6 Using strong sewing thread, sew along the pocket lines, leaving long tails of thread at the start and finish of each line. Strengthen the pockets and secure the threads by knotting each pair of tails firmly, then threading them into the eye of a sewing needle and taking them into the hem (at the top) or the seam allowance (at the bottom).

7 Thread one end of the cord through the button shank and sew it firmly in place.

8 Sewing through the shank, sew the button to one edge of the back of the roll, about halfway up the pockets, with the cord lying across the roll. Roll up the needle roll from the opposite end, then wrap the cord around the roll and secure it by wrapping it around the button a few times.

Thimble pincushion necklace

Out yourself as a sewist with a necklace that's useful as well as cute. ("Useful?" I hear you say: these pincushions are great when you are pinning for fit on a dress form or friend.) It's super-easy, quick, and thrifty to make, a great way of putting widely available and sweet sewing lovelies to good use, and the best gift for sewist friends. What more could you want?

YOU'RE GOING TO NEED...

- 2in (5cm) of craft wire
- Thimble
- Epoxy glue
- 1½in (4cm) diameter circle of velvet
- Strong sewing thread
- Hand-sewing needle
- Polyester stuffing
- Ribbon for necklace: I used ¼in (6mm) wide velvet ribbon

WHAT KIND OF FABRIC?

Velvet is good because it doesn't show pin marks, but if the pincushion is going to be jewelry only, then you can use any fabric that isn't thick or stiff. I have found that a 4in (10cm) circle is about right for an average-size thimble.

1 Bend and twist the wire to form a loop with a twisted neck and curly feet, as shown.

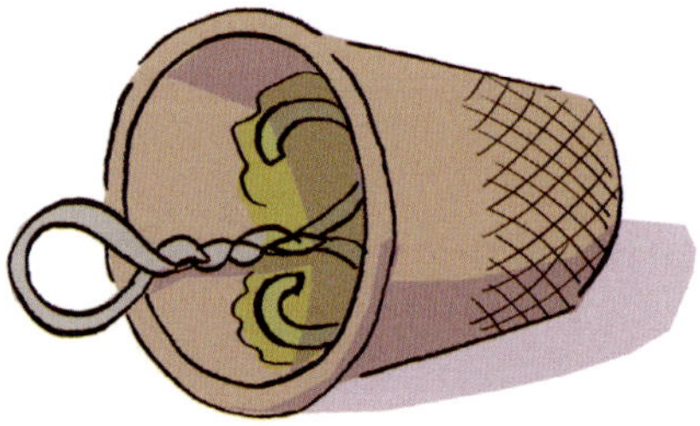

2 Press the curly feet inside the thimble so that they bend to fit against the side, then set the loop aside. Mix up a dollop of epoxy glue (follow the packet instructions) and put it in the thimble against what will be the back side. Press the curly feet into the glue, so that just the loop protrudes above the rim of the thimble, and let dry.

HUNT THE THIMBLE

One thing you have to remember when looking for a thimble to make this pincushion is that any decoration needs to work when the thimble is, in effect, upside down. Lots of thimbles have motifs that are the right way up when the thimble is on your finger; so something like a bird can look very odd (and very dead) lying on its back, feet in the air, around your neck.

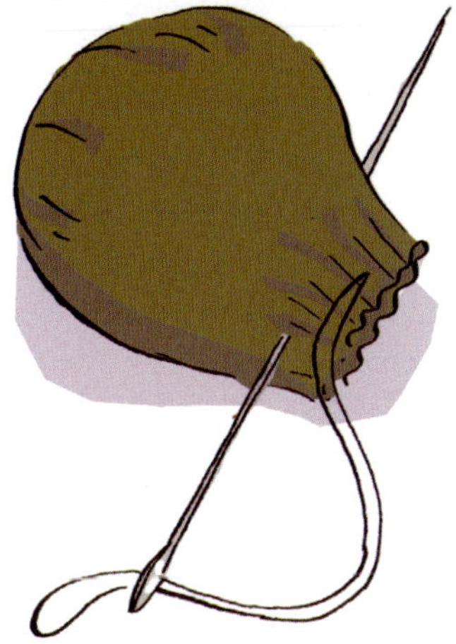

3 Using doubled strong sewing thread, work a line of small running stitches around the edge of the velvet circle.

4 Put a ball of stuffing in the center of the circle and pull the gathers up around it. Add more stuffing if need be to make the pincushion as firm as you want it (I like mine to be really quite firm indeed).

5 Pull the gathers up as tight as possible and stitch back and forth through them to secure them. Cut the thread short.

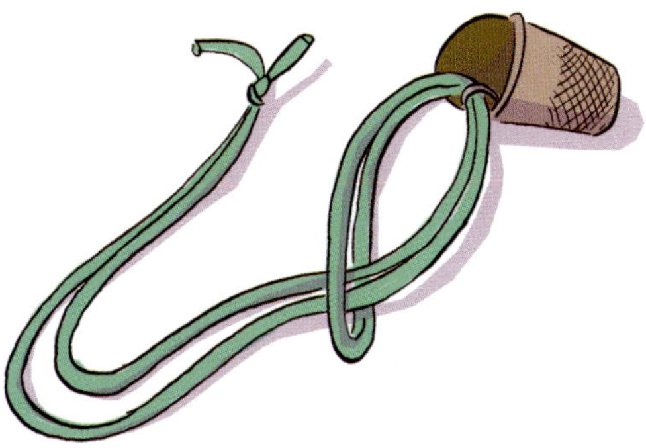

6 Mix up a little more epoxy glue and spread it inside the thimble. Press the stuffed velvet ball down into the thimble, as shown, and let dry. Loop the ribbon through the wire loop and tie the ends to make a necklace the length you prefer.

Techniques

On the following pages you'll find the basic sewing techniques that you will need for the patterns in this book.

TRANSFERRING DESIGNS ONTO FABRIC

On pages 90–94 are the templates for some of the projects in this book, and you'll need to transfer them onto fabric if you want to copy a project exactly.

If you only need the outline of a shape, then just enlarge the template to the right size on a photocopier (all the templates give the correct enlargement percentage), and cut it out. Pin it to the fabric. If you're used to cutting out patterns, or it's a fairly simple shape, just cut out around the edges of the template. Otherwise, draw around it with a fading fabric marker pen (don't be tempted to use an ordinary pen or pencil, as they can permanently mark and spoil your project), then remove the template and cut out the shape.

If there are marks within the template that you need, remember to transfer them onto the fabric, too.

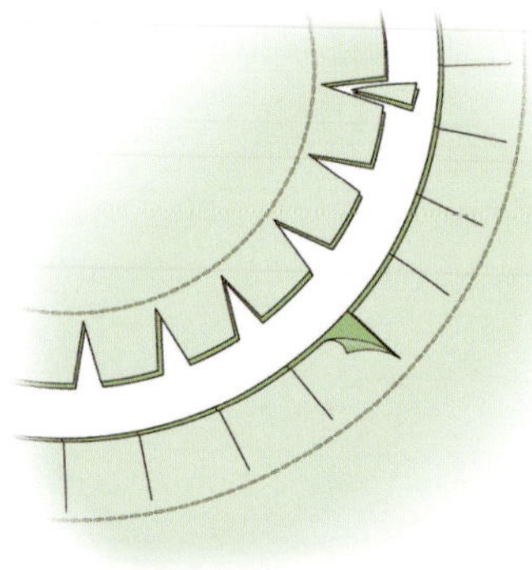

CLIPPING CURVED SEAM ALLOWANCES

This helps curved seams lie flat and will make a real difference to the look of your finished project.

Use the tips of your fabric scissors (don't use tiny embroidery scissors as this will dull the blades) to cut into the seam allowance after stitching, taking great care not to cut through any of the stitches. Seams that curve outward need wedge-shaped notches cut into the seam allowance, while for seams that will curve inward, little slits will do (though I usually just cut notches in both types of seam).

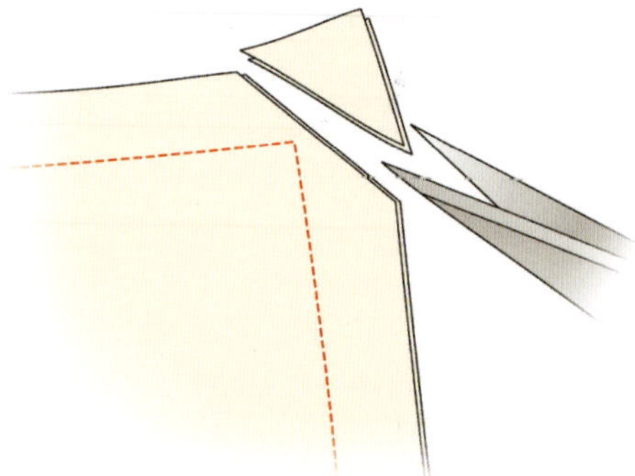

TRIMMING CORNERS

For corners, you need to snip off the excess fabric across the point before you turn the project right side out, so that the finished corner is neat and square. Cut off the fabric across the corner about ⅛in (3mm) away from the stitching, taking care not to cut through the stitches.

TURNING TUBES RIGHT SIDE OUT

When making loops or straps, you can use a loop turner to turn the tube right side out. Alternatively, follow this method, using a needle and thread.

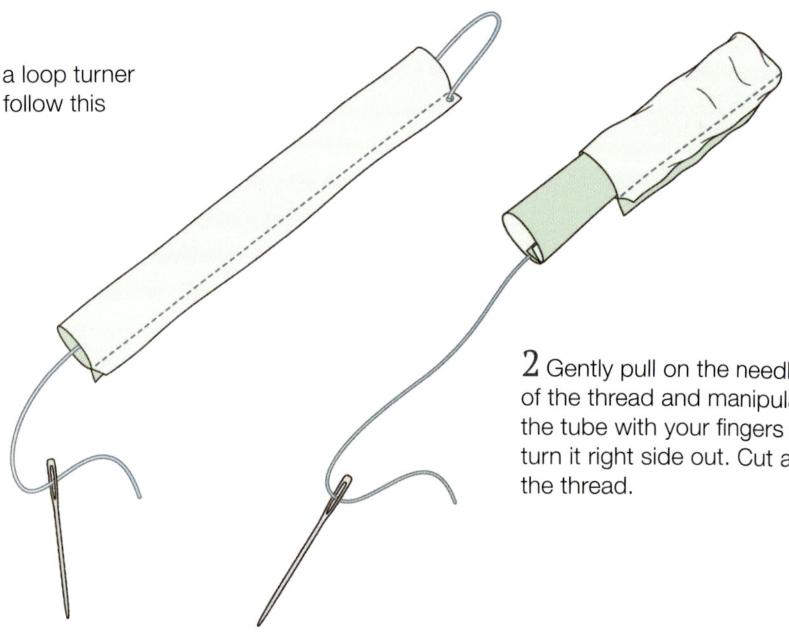

1 Thread a blunt-tipped needle (such as a tapestry needle) with a length of strong sewing thread longer than the tube. Knot one end and take it through the seam allowance close to one end of the tube.

2 Gently pull on the needle end of the thread and manipulate the tube with your fingers to turn it right side out. Cut away the thread.

Stitches

These are the embroidery and utility hand stitches used in the projects.

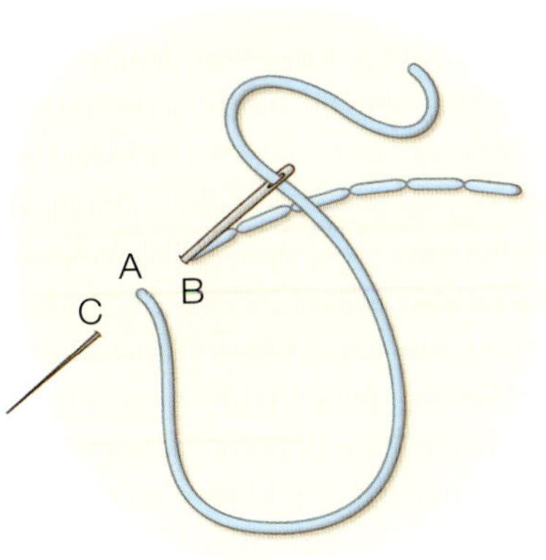

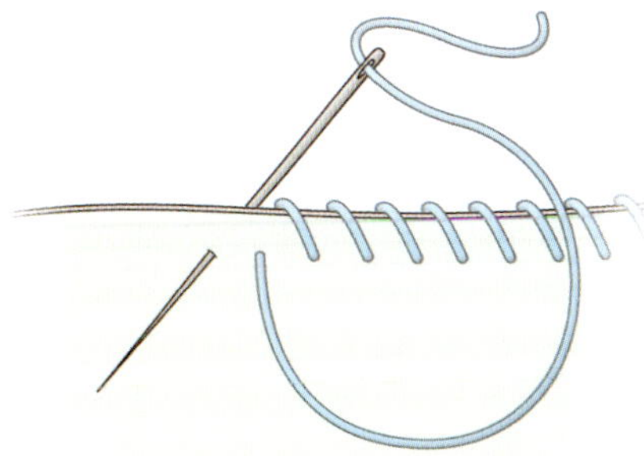

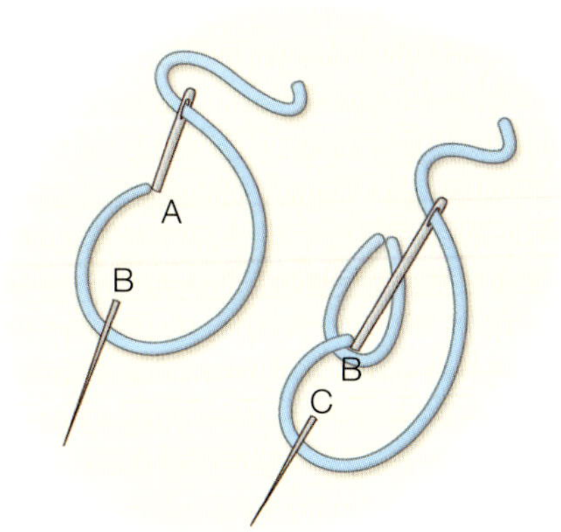

BACKSTITCH

Before the sewing machine was invented, this is what you used to sew up seams. And it's a versatile embroidery stitch.

Working from right to left, bring the needle up at A, down at B, and up at C, one stitch length ahead of A. For the next stitch, go down at A and come up a stitch length ahead of C, and continue along in this way.

WHIP STITCH

This is used to join fabrics either right sides or wrong sides together. Hold together the two pieces of fabric, matching the edges to be joined. From the back, take the needle through both pieces, close to the edge. Take the needle over the edges and to the back and through both pieces again a short distance further along, pulling the thread taut to complete the stitch. If you are joining the fabrics wrong sides together, you can hide the starting knot between the layers.

CHAIN STITCH

This is a marvelous stitch—easy to work, forgiving of inexperience, and very good-looking.

Bring the needle up at A, then insert it at the same point. Make a short stitch to B, looping the thread under the tip of the needle.

Pull the thread through to form the first loop in the chain. Insert the needle at B again and make another short stitch to C (the same length as the A to B stitch), then loop the thread under the tip of the needle. Continue, keeping all the stitches the same length. To anchor the last stitch in the chain, take the needle down just outside the loop, forming a little bar over it.

BLANKET STITCH

Another stitch that's both utility and decorative. Use it to sew one piece of fabric to another, or just as an embroidery stitch, or work it along an edge, or use it to join two edges.

Bring the needle up at A, down at B, and up at C (directly below B), looping the thread under the tip of the needle. Pull the needle through, then insert it at D and bring it out at E, again looping the thread under the tip.

If you are working it along an edge, the principle is the same, but the horizontal bar of thread lies along the edge of the fabric, as shown.

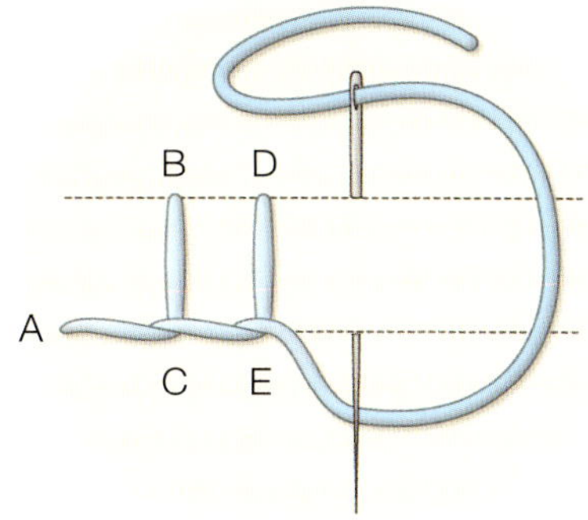

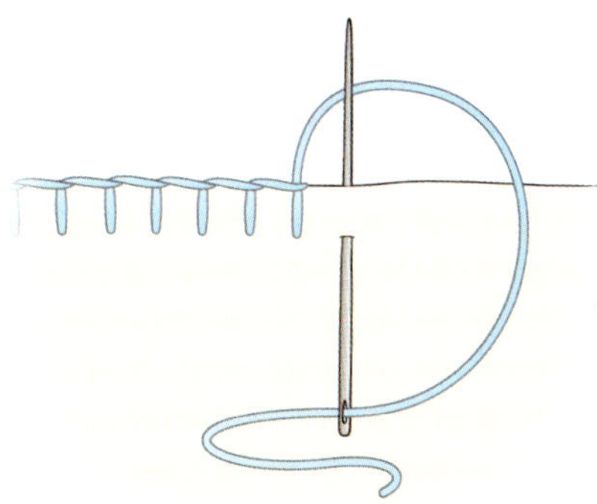

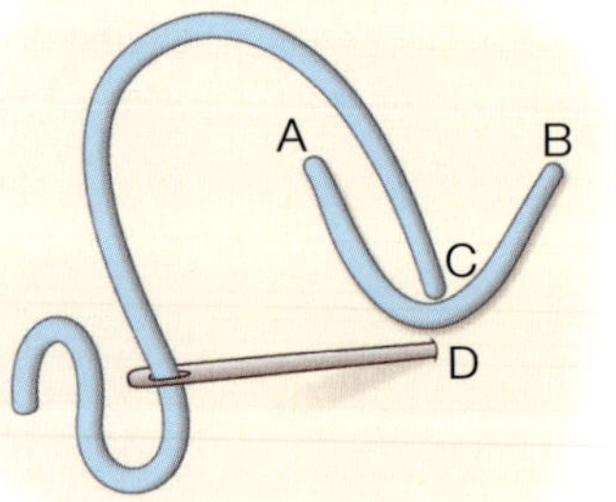

FLY STITCH

As well as being great for stitching down buttons decoratively (see Yo-yo storage pouch step 9, page 36), fly stitch is also a lovely embroidery stitch.

Bring the needle up at A and down at B, leaving a loop of thread. Bring the needle up inside the loop at C and pull the loop taut, then take the needle down at D, outside the loop. The C to D stitch can be long or short, as you prefer.

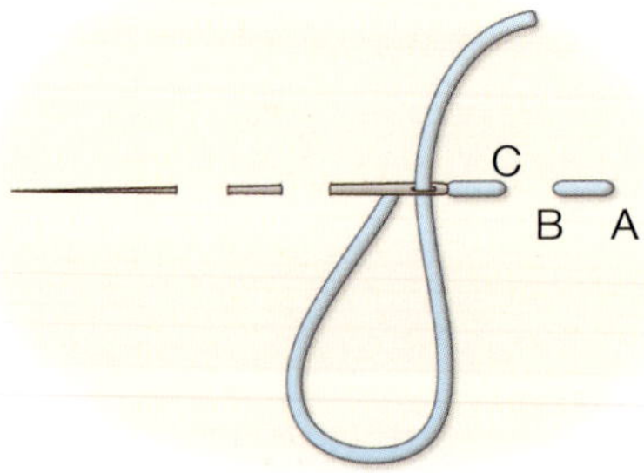

RUNNING STITCH

Another multi-purpose stitch: use it for basting (not worrying about stitch length or tidiness), for decoration, or for gathering.

Bring the needle up at A, down at B, and up at C, and continue in this way. If being used decoratively, you can space the stitches evenly and make them all the same length, or work them more randomly, depending on the look you want.

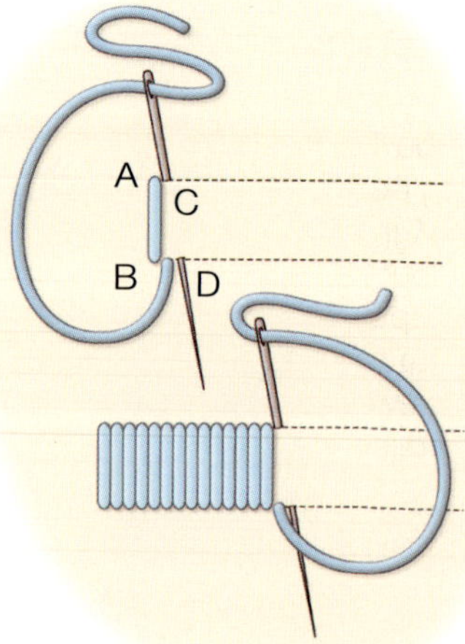

SATIN STITCH

The secret of success with this stitch is getting the tension right. You can outline the shape to be satin stitched with split stitch (see right), which gives a defined edge that's easier to keep neat than if you just follow a drawn outline.

Bring the needle up at A, down at B, up at C, down at D, and so on, working the stitches close together so that no fabric shows in between them.

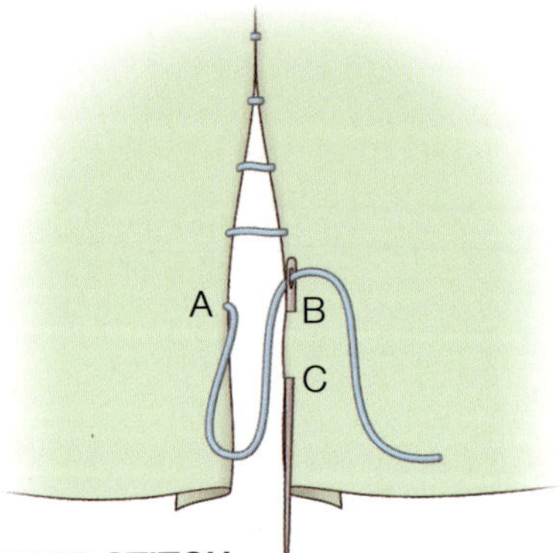

LADDER STITCH

This is the best stitch for closing up the gap in a machine- or hand-sewn seam once the project has been turned right side out.

Turn in the seam allowances across the gap and press them (with your fingers or an iron). Bring the needle up through the pressed fold at A, then take it straight across the gap to B. Make a tiny stitch through the folded edge and bring it back to the front at C. Continue in this way, zigzagging from one side to another and making the stitches equally spaced.

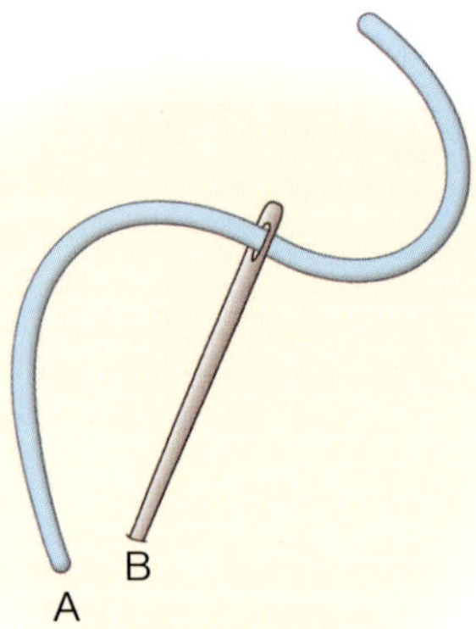

STAB STITCH

Yet another stitch that's both utility and decorative.

Simply bring the needle up at A and take it down at B, making a short, straight stitch.

Crochet

Granny squares

If you want to include granny squares in the Damp-proof picnic mat project on page 41, then this is the pattern I used. I chose a worsted-weight (Aran) yarn and used a G/6 (4.5mm) crochet hook. Note that the pattern is worked using American terminology; see the list of abbreviations below for UK equivalents.

Ch 6. Join with a sl st to form a ring.
Round 1: Ch 3, this counts as the first dc. Work 2 more dc into ring, [ch 3, 3 dc into ring] 3 times. Ch 3, sl st to join to beginning of round. *12 dc*
Join a new color to any ch-3 space using a sl st.
Round 2: Ch 3, this counts as the first dc. 2 dc, ch 3, 3 dc into same space, ch 1 [3 dc, ch 3, 3 dc in next 3-ch space, ch 1] 3 times. Sl st to join to beginning of round. *24 dc*
Join a new color to any ch-3 space using a sl st.
Round 3: Ch 3, this counts as the first dc. 2 dc, ch 3, 3 dc into same space, ch 1 [3 dc, ch 3, 3 dc in next 1-ch space, ch 1, 3 dc, ch 3, 3 dc in next 3-ch space] 3 times. Sl st to join to beginning of round. *36 dc*
Continue in the same way—working 3 dc into every 1-ch space in the previous round, and two lots of 3 dc separated by 3 ch into each corner space—until the square is as large as you want it to be.
Work one round of sc all around the finished square: this will act as the seam allowance.

CROCHET ABBREVIATIONS

US	UK
dc double crochet	**tr** treble crochet
sc single crochet	**dc** double crochet
sl st slip stitch	**ss** slip stitch

Templates

This section contains all the templates you will need. Where a template is not given at actual size, simply photocopy it at the percentage indicated in order to enlarge it. See page 86 for how to transfer the template designs onto fabric.

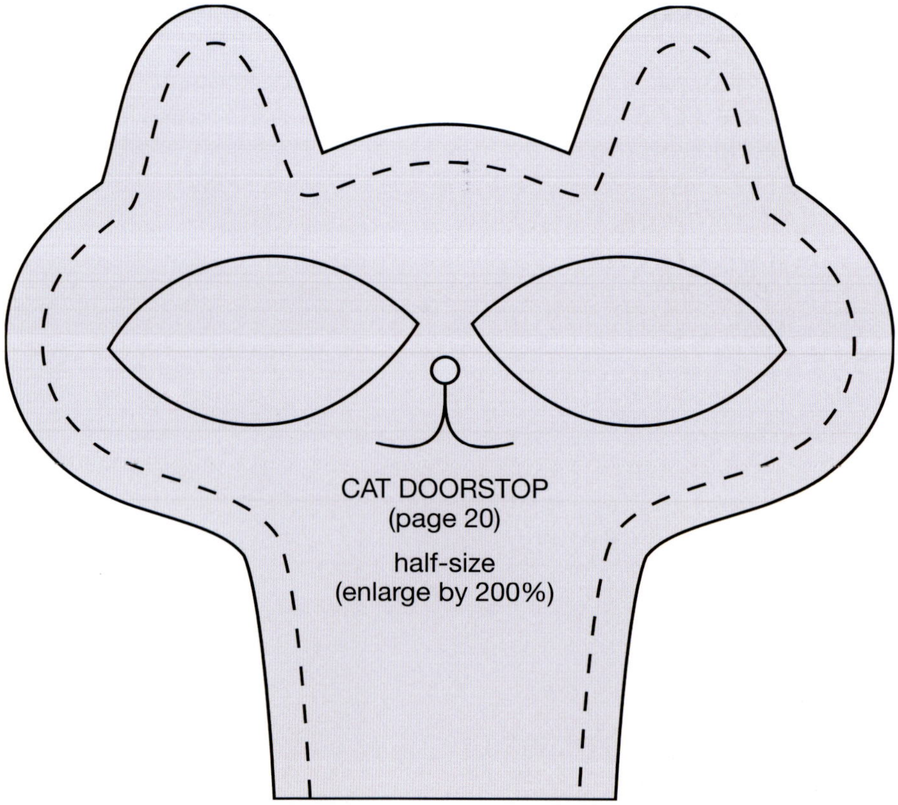

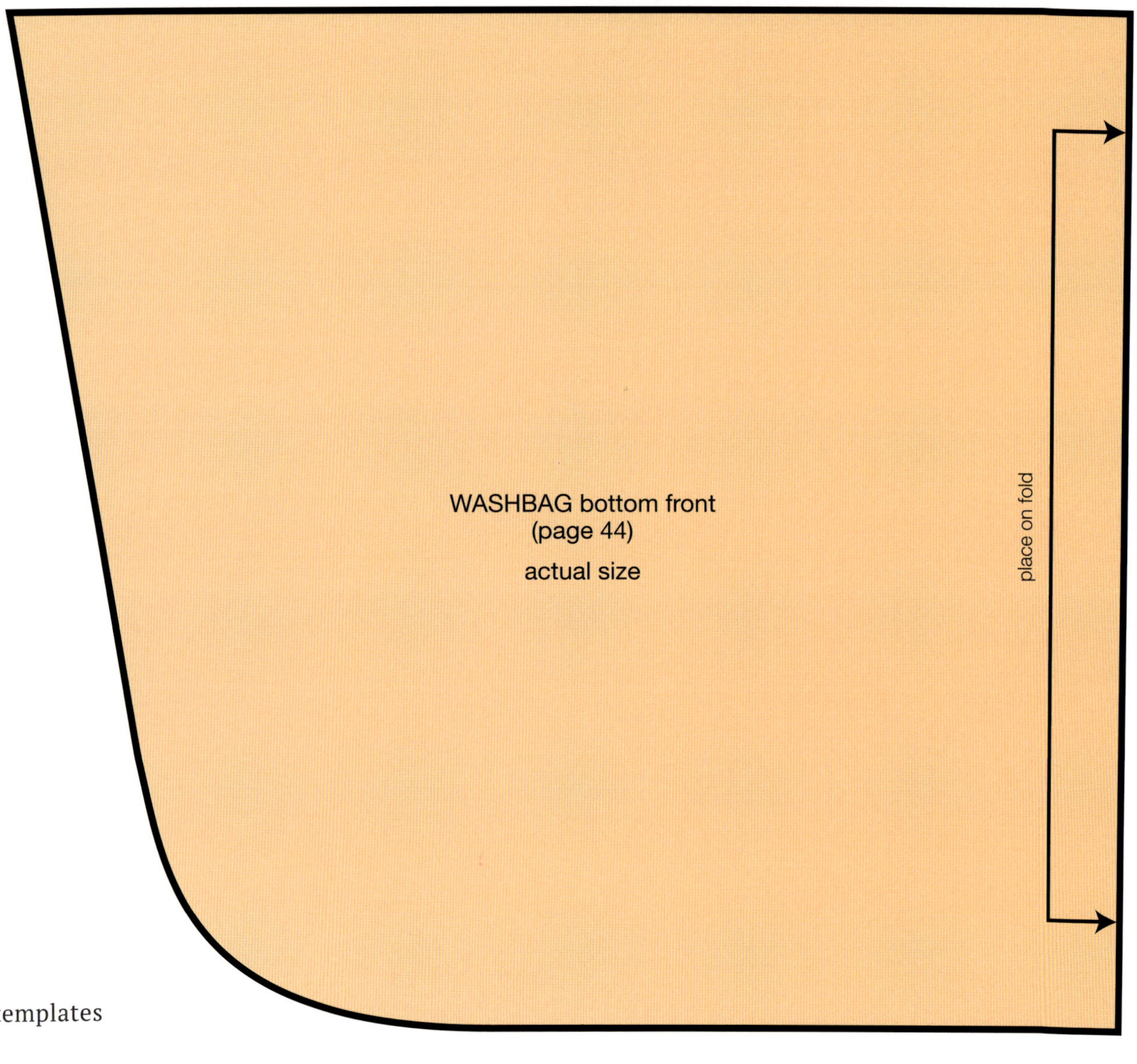

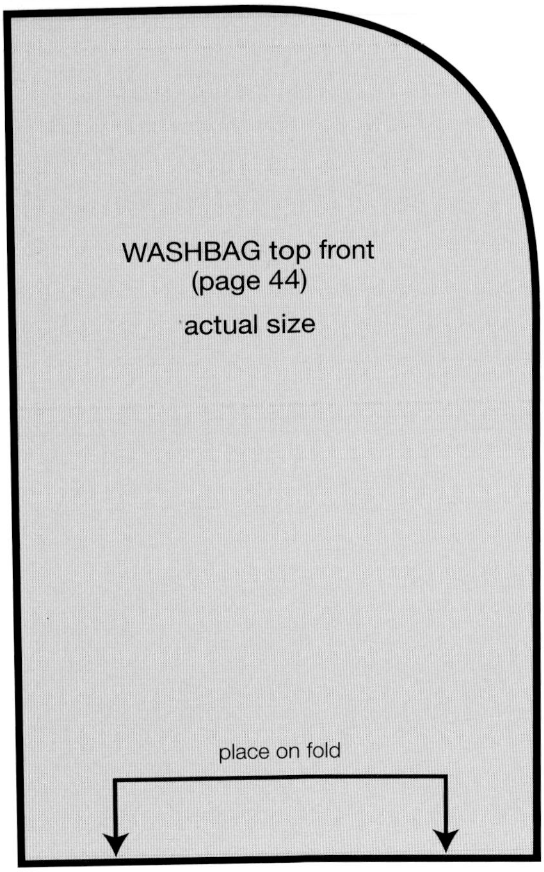
WASHBAG top front
(page 44)
actual size
place on fold

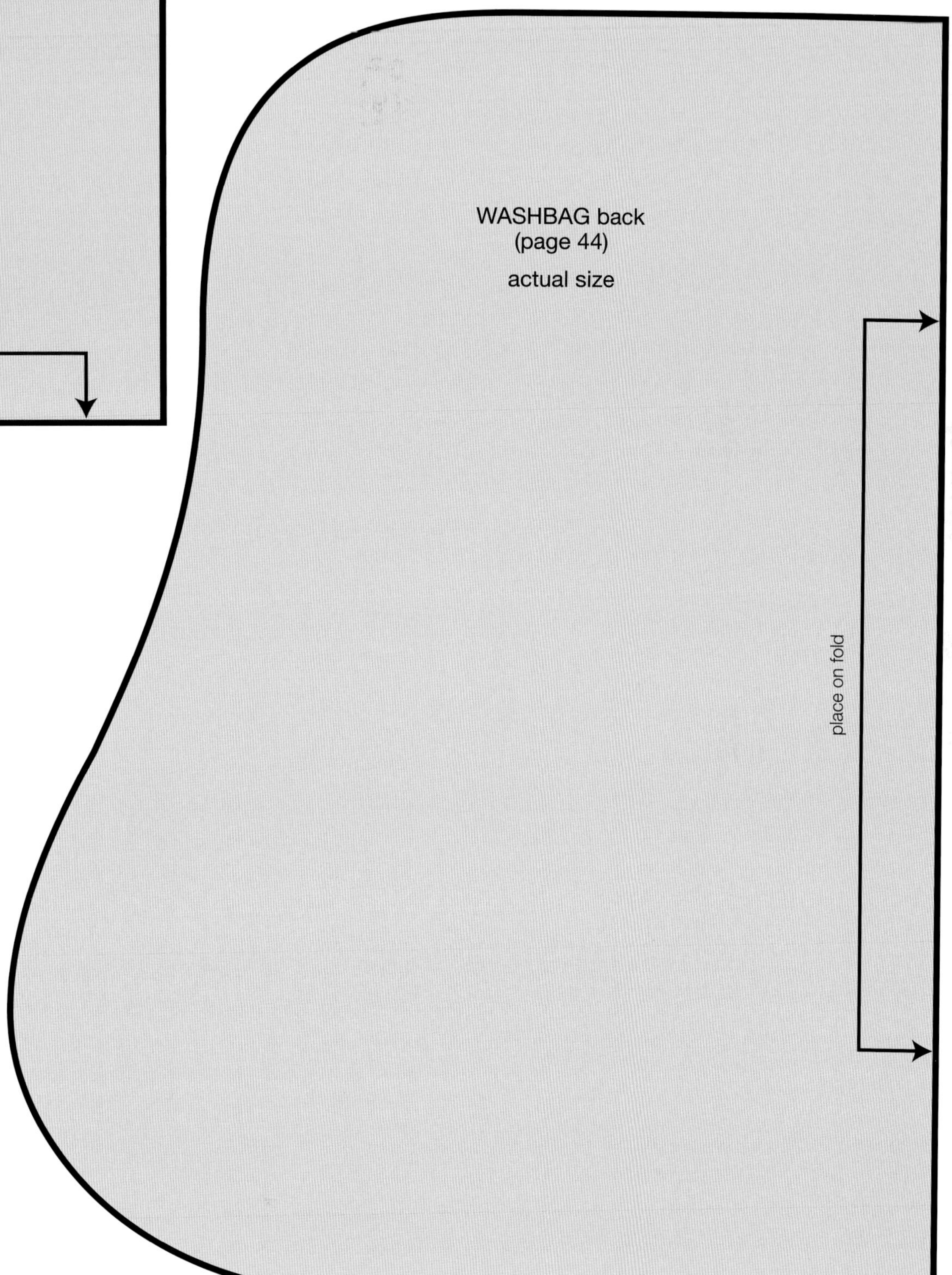
WASHBAG back
(page 44)
actual size
place on fold

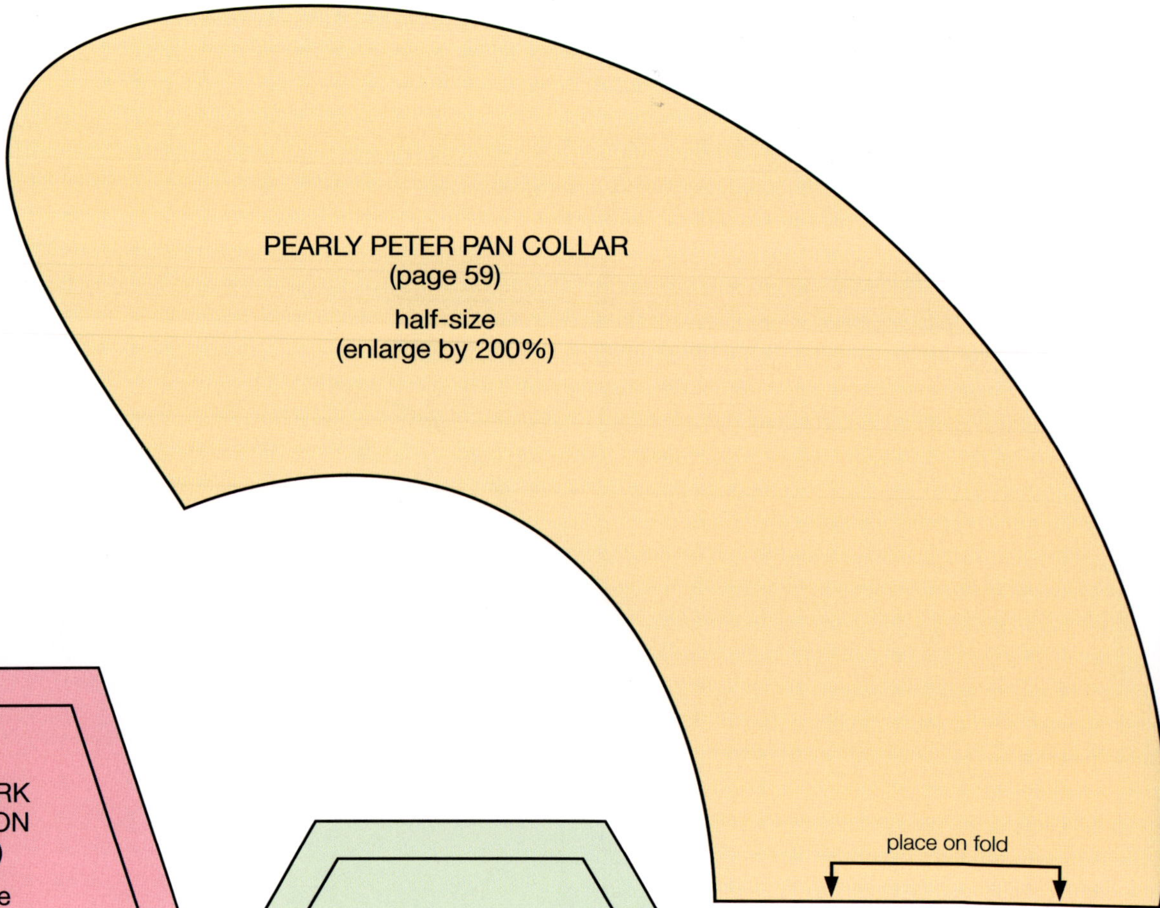
PEARLY PETER PAN COLLAR
(page 59)
half-size
(enlarge by 200%)
place on fold

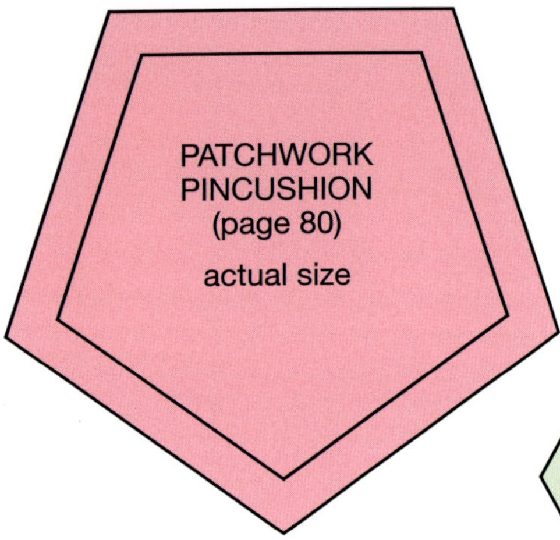
PATCHWORK
PINCUSHION
(page 80)
actual size

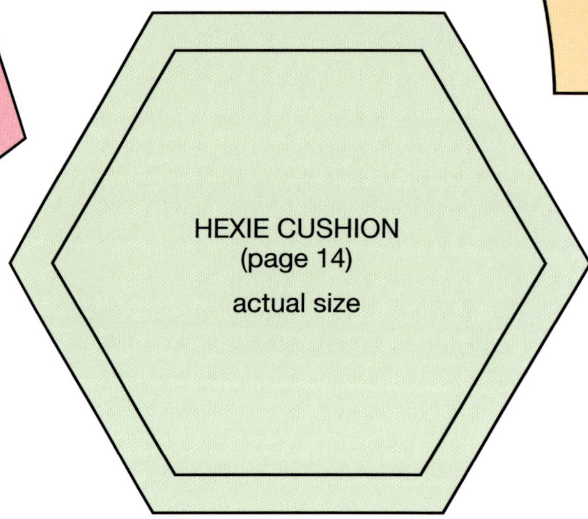
HEXIE CUSHION
(page 14)
actual size

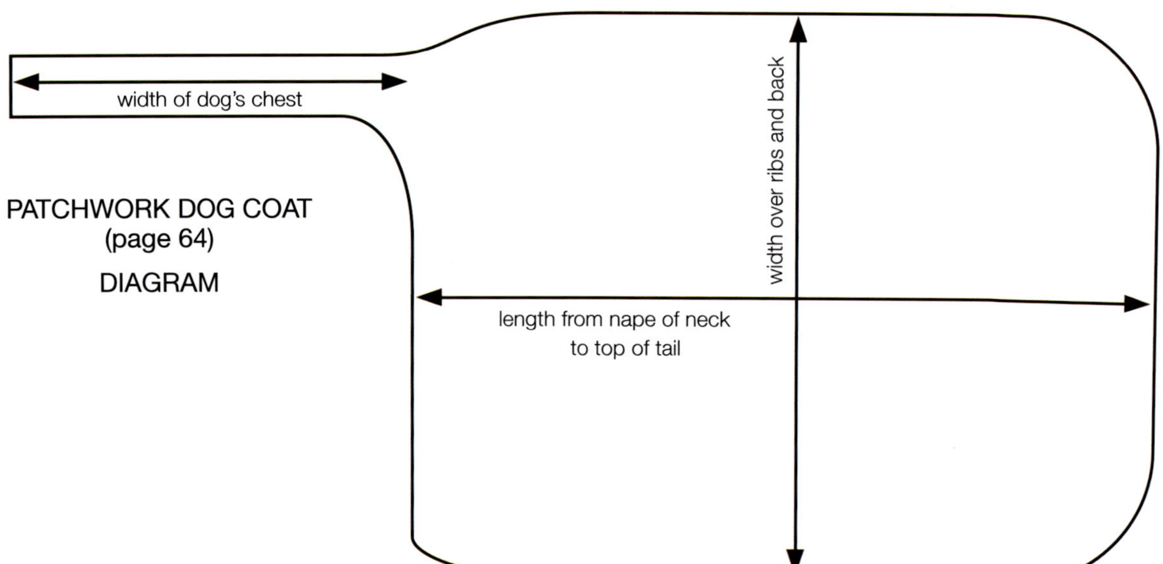
width of dog's chest
PATCHWORK DOG COAT
(page 64)
DIAGRAM
width over ribs and back
length from nape of neck
to top of tail

SAUSAGE DOG DRAFT EXCLUDER
(page 23)

all pieces are half-size
(enlarge by 200%)

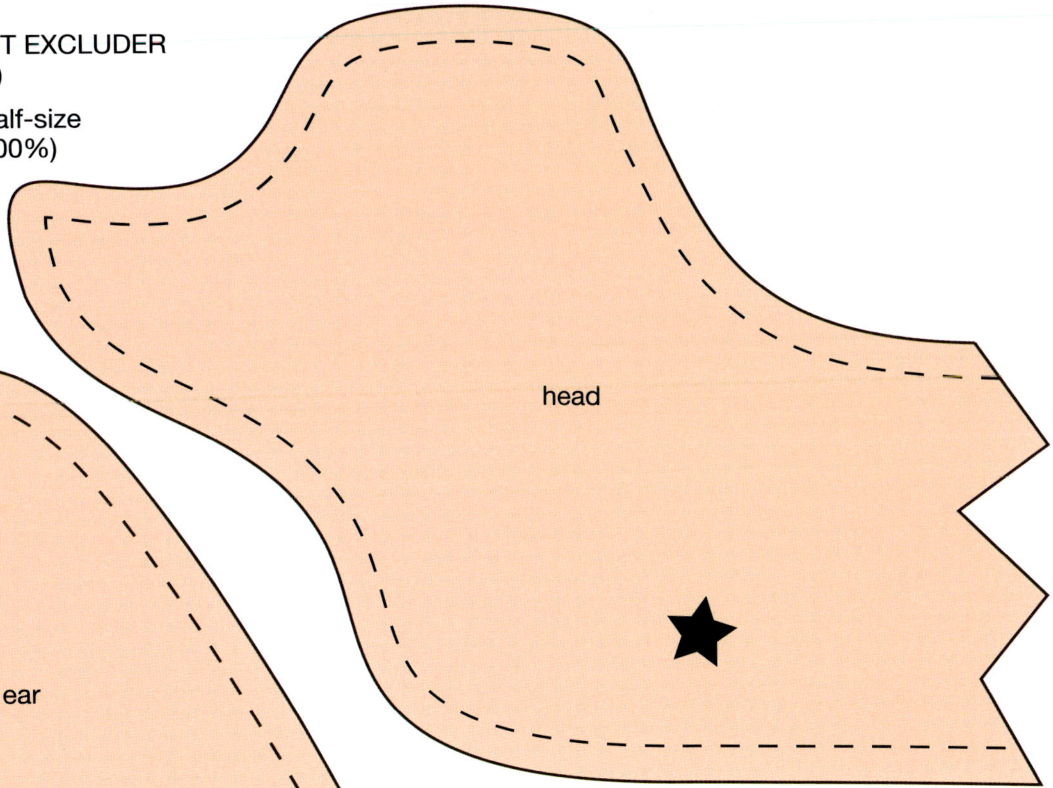

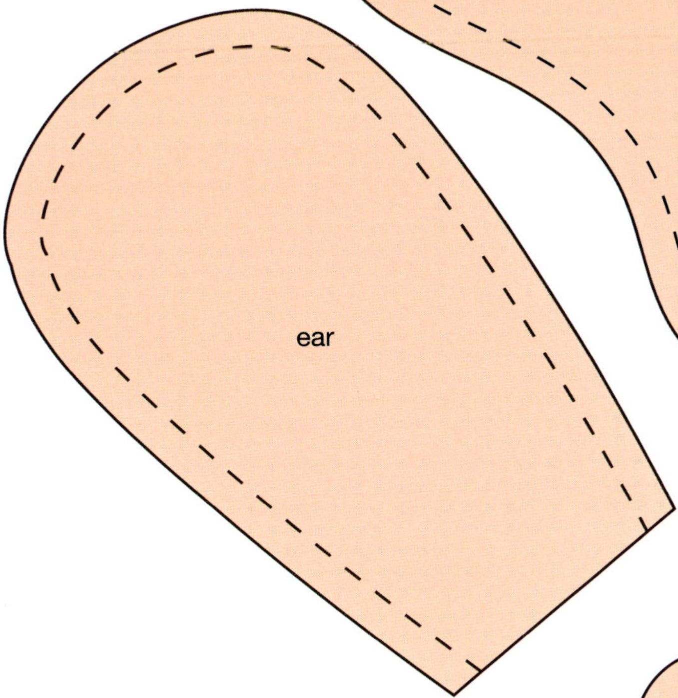

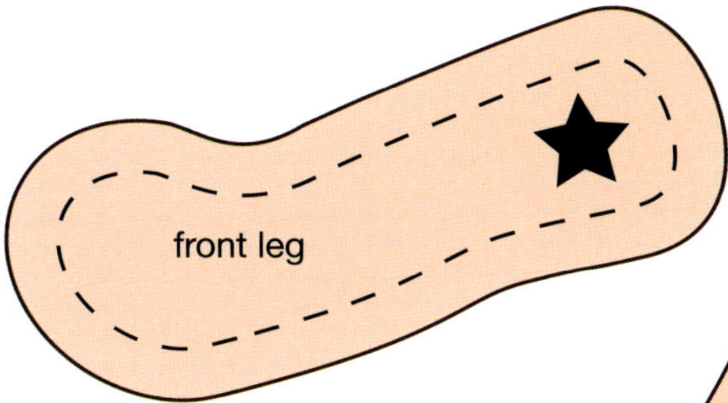

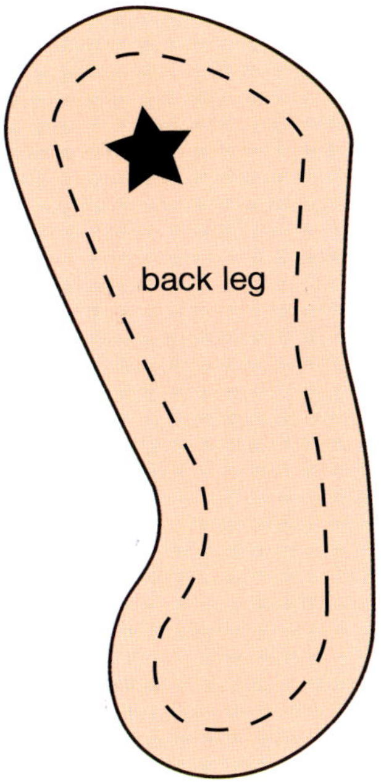

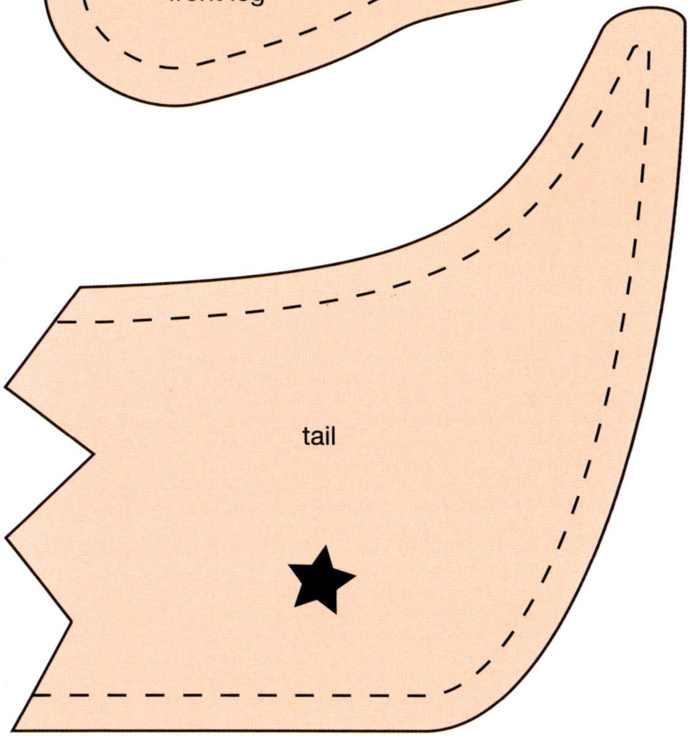

YO-YO STORAGE POUCH
(page 34)
half-size
(enlarge by 200%)

Suppliers

US

Fabricland
www.fabricland.com

J&O Fabrics
www.jandofabrics.com

Michaels
www.michaels.com

Hobby Lobby
www.hobbylobby.com

Purl Soho
www.purlsoho.com

UK

Guthrie & Ghani
www.guthrie-ghani.co.uk
Lovely fabrics and haberdashery, and lovely staff.

John Lewis
www.johnlewis.com
Great sewing equipment and some fabrics.

Liberty
www.libertylondon.com
Lovely fabrics.

Fabrics Galore
www.fabricsgalore.co.uk
Always my first stop on a fabric shop. Great range at excellent prices.

Creative Quilting
www.creativequilting.co.uk
Good range of fabrics and very helpful staff. Also sell some embroidery floss and sewing equipment.

Cloth House
www.clothhouse.com
My favorite fabric shop, with a range of acrylic/wool mix felts.

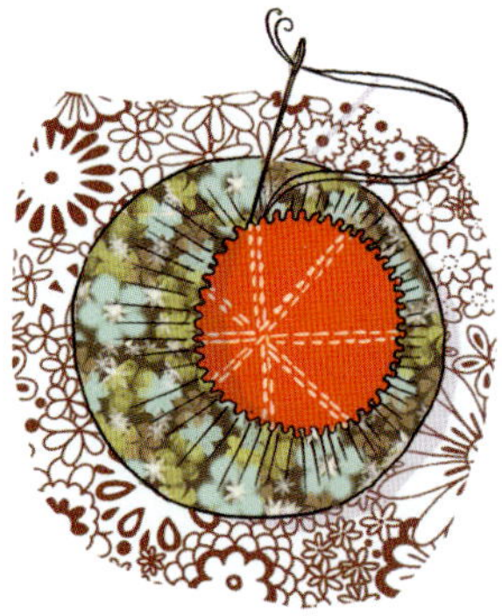

Acknowledgments

My thanks to Cindy Richards at CICO for continuing to give me the opportunity to make books, and to Carmel Edmonds for keeping everything on track. Thank you to Katie Hardwicke for her efficient and accurate editorial work; to Sania Pell, Luis Peral, Catherine Woram, Jo Henderson, and Penny Wincer for the lovely photographs and styling; and to Michael Hill, Carrie Hill, and Stephen Dew for their illustrations. Thanks, as ever, to Philip for the food.

Index